ADVANCE PRAISE FOR

Read Matthew to Live Your Life, Read John to Save Your Soul

I can't get through the first two pages without crying. God's spirit is all over this book, and I am meant to read it!

—MONICA FALBO,
dental hygienist

This book is so simple, and so clear, that it makes the message of Christ easy to understand for everyone. How to live your life, and how to save your soul—what more do you need?

—CHAPLAIN BOB MILLER,
Ocala Farm Ministry

I recommend Dr. Kindred's book to anyone who has the desire to gain a fuller, more tangible understanding of the words of Jesus Christ. The author's very personal account of his own experiences may give others a point of reference in their own lives.

—LOU ANGORA,
executive producer, Morning Light Films

Read Matthew
to Live Your

Life, Read John
to Save Your
Soul

The Best Advice I Ever Got

DOUGLAS KINDRED

WESTBOW
PRESS®
A DIVISION OF THOMAS NELSON
& ZONDERVAN

WestBow Press books may be ordered through booksellers or by contacting:

WestBow Press
A Division of Thomas Nelson & Zondervan
1663 Liberty Drive
Bloomington, IN 47403
www.westbowpress.com
1 (866) 928-1240

ISBN: 978-1-4908-3587-7 (sc)
ISBN: 978-1-4908-3586-0 (hc)
ISBN: 978-1-4908-3588-4 (e)

Library of Congress Control Number: 2014907758

Print information available on the last page.

WestBow Press rev. date: 03/29/2016

To my sons, Kai and Mitchell,

the secret to life and to eternity is in this book.
You must read it and understand it, and mostly you must live it.

Special thanks to Mom and Dad ... and
Tina for their love and support.

CONTENTS

CHAPTER 1

The Rise and Fall of an Ordinary Man

There is a way which seemeth right unto a man,
but the end thereof are the ways of death.
—PROVERBS 14:12

THE RISE

I was born in the heartland of America in the small town of Lincoln, Illinois, in 1961. My father, Tom, was a barber, and my mother, Judy, was a schoolteacher. They were fantastic parents and did a great job raising my brother, sister, and me.

Dad was a hardworking man. He eventually got into food service and managing cafeterias to make more money to support and provide for the family. He was good at it and was frequently transferred to new accounts, so we moved around a lot. This was good, as we got to experience different people, different places, and different cultures and learn new things. He later started his own very successful racehorse equipment business all through determination, hard work, and treating his customers well.

Dad worked hard and taught us kids to work hard. He taught me things a man needs to know—how to shoot a gun, catch a fish, ride a horse, change a tire and change the oil, build a fence, and negotiate a deal, and mostly he taught me how to work hard.

Mom took care of us, provided a wonderful and loving home environment, loved us, nurtured us, taught us, fed us, and gave us the greatest foundation anyone could have in life. She gave us a foundation on the Rock of Jesus Christ. She took us to church, took us to Sunday school, sent us to vacation Bible school and church camp in the summers, and taught us about faith through her strong, unwavering example. By the way, I didn't like any of that stuff, but it turned out to be the most important thing in my life. At the age of fifteen I was born again and accepted Jesus Christ as my Lord and my Savior.

So as a result of this wonderful upbringing and my own personality, I worked very hard. I worked hard at everything I did—school, track, racing horses, working in the watermelon fields of South Alabama, and later as a framing carpenter. I went to college at East Tennessee State University to study physics and math, and with a lot of hard work, I graduated with a 3.99 GPA. I then went on to graduate school and worked harder to earn my doctorate in optics (the physics of light) at the Institute of Optics at University of Rochester in Rochester, New York. After that I took a job at my professor's company, Gradient Lens Corporation, in Rochester, where I worked even harder. I eventually became president of this small company, and we grew from employing about six people when I started to about thirty people.

I met a nice girl named Sue while I was in graduate school. She became my wife, and we had two wonderful sons, Kai and Mitch. Life was good, and we were living the middle-class American dream.

THE FALL—DRIFTING AWAY

But a bad thing happened. During all this time I eventually started drifting away from God. You see, when I was younger, I had a fantastic foundation given to me by my mother. That foundation carried me through college and graduate school pretty well, but as time went on, I spent less and less time in prayer, less and less time reading the Bible, and almost no time attending church. I was too busy, working. I eventually forgot about God, about my need for God and having a relationship with Him, and completely neglected to put Him first in my life. Instead, I was striving to do it all on my own, in my own strength, and through my own efforts.

In his book *The Danger of Drifting*,[1] Dr. David Jeremiah says, "It is so easy to fall prey to the busyness of life and lose our perspective on Christ. When we become preoccupied with life to the extent that we have little time to develop our spiritual core, drifting is inevitable." Yes, that is exactly what I did.

Throughout my life I have generally been a positive, happy guy, always loved other people, helped others, and enjoyed life. But for about the last twenty years I became so overwhelmed with work and life that I was very stressed. I didn't even realize that it was all because I had drifted away from God, lost my focus, and lost my priorities. I was not living the life God intended for me, but instead I was trying to be independent of Him and make my own way. The result was eventually devastating.

I put my work ahead of everything, including my wife, and I ended up separated after twelve years of marriage and two kids. We eventually got divorced. It was hard on everyone—me, my wife, and the boys. As Billy Graham[2] says, "Every divorce represents a broken dream, a shattered hope, a ruined expectation." I am saddened to see anyone go through a divorce.

Still in spite of this, I remained positive and generally happy, and I thought life was pretty good. I still had my job, so I kept on working, kept on striving. I had a nice little house on Lake Ontario, did some fishing, dated a couple nice young ladies, enjoyed a lot of quality time with my kids, taking them to Boy Scouts, hockey, lacrosse, swimming, etc. I must say I was a bit oblivious to my own failure. Though I was saddened by it, I didn't let it change me. I kept on working, striving actually, and still ignoring God. In other words, this tremendous loss in my life still didn't wake me up.

After that God tried to nudge me awake a couple more times, having two car accidents at sixty miles per hour within a year, both on the same road. In both cases someone ran a stop sign in front of me before I even had time to hit the brakes. I survived, and I was not seriously injured. That should've woken me up, but it didn't.

The First Sign

God gave me two signs that something was going to happen, but once again I was too clueless, too oblivious to understand. The first sign came in the spring of 2010 I kept repeatedly hearing a voice, God's voice saying, "Give away everything you own and be ready." I could not get this voice out of my head. It was there all day every day for months. Yet I ignored it. I mean really— It sounds crazy, right? Why would I want to give away all my possessions? I have never been considered a materialistic man. I do enjoy nice things, but I have never been one for expensive cars, houses, boats, etc. Just normal sort of suburban American possessions— a Ford Taurus, a Ford F-150, some clothes, nice furniture, some art, books, lots of tools in the garage, some sporting goods, a small boat, and a canoe. It was all nice but nothing extravagant by any means. Yet I liked my stuff, especially my books, tools, sporting goods, and of course the nice leather couch and TV. So I ignored this pesky voice in my head—God's voice. That really was not a smart thing to do.

The Second Sign

One morning before work I received a call from Mom. She was very upset, crying and sobbing. It was difficult to understand her. She told me that I had to get out of my house and that I had to get out now! She had a dream, a vision, that she saw God raining fire down on my house. I didn't listen. Instead, I calmed her down. Told her everything would be fine, that I was fine, that if there was a fire, I could easily get out, and that I had good fire insurance. I was an idiot.

The Chastening

Mom was right, of course. She always is. She knows God. He talks to her, and she listens—unlike me, her foolish son. About a month or two later God rained down fire on my house.

It was not literal fire. That would have been much easier to handle. It was in the form of mold. My lovely little lake house got moldy, very moldy. After all, it's cool, dark, and damp on Lake Ontario—perfect conditions for mold growth. Everything I owned got moldy, everything. I could literally see mold growing on my nice leather couch and chair, on my clothes in the closet, on my belt in the dresser drawer, on my shoes on the floor, on backs of pictures hanging on the wall, and on my books. (I had a wonderful collection of books—travel narratives from the 1910s to the 1930s, adventures in Africa, the Amazon, Mongolia, etc.)

The house got moldy. All my possessions got very moldy, and I became very sick. It started on July 1, 2010, with a bad cough, mild headache, mild earache, and extreme fatigue. It just felt like a cold. I thought surely I would get over it in a week or so.

After three weeks of getting progressively worse, I went to see my doctor. I was given some antibiotics and sent on my way. After two more weeks I had gotten much worse, so I went back to the doctor, was given more antibiotics, and continued to go downhill. I went back to the doctor and kept asking if mold could be the issue. They didn't think so, but they tested me for mold allergies anyway, found that to be negative, and said that I probably just had a virus and that I would get over it. The cough persisted and worsened for sixteen weeks, and my health went continually and severely downhill during that time. When I say I was sick (and it was from the mold), I had the following twelve symptoms listed roughly in their order of severity:

1. Extreme debilitating fatigue—It was indescribable, not like any other fatigue. No one can really understand this unless they have experienced it. It is not like any other form of exhaustion, not like staying awake for seventy-two hours straight, not like physical or mental or emotional exhaustion. It is very different. I had to sleep. It became literally impossible to stay awake at times, no matter how much I wanted to or needed to stay awake. I was sleeping about fourteen to sixteen hours every night, waking in the morning totally un-refreshed, feeling as if I hadn't slept at all. It took about two hours to really wake up, requiring a full pot of coffee and a lot of calories for breakfast. If I did not leave work early enough, I absolutely could not make the drive home. I'd have to stop the car and sleep on the side of the road. I did this frequently. What was weird was that I would seem fine to everyone at work at two o'clock. By three

o'clock I had to leave, or I would fall asleep right there. I later discovered that my adrenaline level was extremely low.

2. Burning in the brain—I had an intense burning and tingling pain in my head like a thousand hot needles poking into my brain. I had a stiff neck and tingling in the back of the neck and head, sometimes mild, sometimes extreme. Nothing relieved this. Sometimes it was so intense for prolonged periods that I no longer desired to live. This continued for almost two years!

3. No endurance—I was very weak and tired during waking hours. Muscles were relatively strong, but endurance was nonexistent. I could only do physical exercise for one to two minutes. I was normally a pretty fit guy. I would run, swim, cycle, and canoe, and I could typically swim five hundred yards. Now I could only swim fifty.

4. Brain fog—I was in a constant brain fog, working at about 50 percent mental capacity, sometimes as low as 30 percent sometimes as high as 80 percent. Before I had gotten sick, I had been a relatively smart guy. I'm a physicist and businessman and president of the company. I needed my brain, but it became very difficult to think and make any decisions at all.

5. Frequent loss of balance and stumbling—I would get out of the car and literally stumble in to work, work for a while, stumble down the hallway, etc.

6. Constant mild headache in upper right front—This was constant for about the first four months, but then it became intermittent. When I was feeling very sick, it returned. When I was feeling healthier, it went away.

7. Weakness and tingling of muscles, such as face, fingertips, toes, etc., plus major muscle groups—My skin felt like it was crawling all day every day.

8. Diarrhea—I had this constantly for two years. When I'm healthy in Ocala, Florida, (more on that later) it goes away. When I'm sick, it's very bad. The doc told me the reason for this. My sIgA is very low. What that means is my mucous membranes dry up. Therefore, I have no stomach lining and intestinal lining, and whatever I eat is not well digested, making me feel awful.

9. Starving—I was hungry all the time, eating five meals per day. Calories were the only thing that made me feel good.

10. Often cold—When I feel sick, I prefer eighty-degree temperatures. During healthy periods I am happy at seventy-two degrees, but when I'm sick from the mold, that seems very cold.

11. Intolerance to exercise—It makes me feel much worse the next day. Any activity put me out for two to three days. At times I would feel good enough to go outside and try to exercise, and it felt kind of good to do it; however, somewhere between six hours and twenty-four hours later, I would really suffer. My body would turn dark red, hot, prickly, and my eyes would turn pinkish yellow. My liver enzymes were very high.

12. Cough—It was uncontollable for sixteen weeks—nonstop coughing all day. However, when I took large doses of serrapeptase, the cough was gone! When I stop taking it, the cough returned within one day. Even after two and a half years, the cough is still there, just suppressed by the serrapeptase.

I ended up seeing six different doctors, trying to figure this out and get some relief. The first five docs did all kinds of tests and couldn't find anything wrong with me except that my liver enzymes were high, so they kept asking if I had been drinking a lot of alcohol. I hadn't. This went on for two years, and no one was able to help me. One doctor said that I probably have chronic fatigue syndrome and that there is no cure. He said it would probably go away in two to four years and that I would just have to accept it and adjust my lifestyle. In the meantime I did get some relief of my symptoms through an integrative health professional in San Diego who specialized in nutrition, acupuncture, and alternative medicine. A combination of diet, supplements, acupuncture, and other treatments helped to relieve the symptoms a little, but I was not getting better. I was getting worse.

I knew the illness was from the mold in my home, so I tried to clean it, tried to save it, and tried to save my possessions. I spent an absolute fortune on mold remediation in the structure of the home. I also cleaned all my possessions. Actually I was too weak to do anything, so I paid my housekeeper to clean everything repeatedly with bleach. It would be good for a week. Then the mold smell would return. I eventually moved out of the house and stayed at the Marriott. I had nowhere else to go.

I couldn't afford it, but I was so sick that I could not care for myself. I was too weak to shop, cook, clean, do laundry, etc. The staff at the Marriott in Rochester was very kind and gracious and took good care of me. I eventually got a brand-new apartment and new furniture. It didn't help. I was still sick and getting sicker.

These symptoms persisted for two years, continuing to worsen the entire time. There were several nights when I expected to die before morning. I had lost my health, and eventually I lost everything—my house, my vehicles, all my possessions, my money. Even my ex-wife lost her job, and she and children moved to Connecticut. The only thing I had left was my job, and as I had gotten worse, I was only able to work two to four hours per day and only at about 30 to 50 percent of my normal mental capacity.

I became very desperate. During the little time that I was awake and coherent, I read all I could about mold-related illness to try to get some help. Many of you have heard of black mold poisoning, but it happens with other molds as well. I found a lot of people with the same symptoms, but with virtually no help from the medical community. For the most part, the medical community seems to deny that this problem even exists. It is very frustrating. The worst part was the tingling and burning pain in my brain. That was almost constant for two years and at times was so intense I just wanted to die to alleviate the pain.

Finally the sixth doctor I saw explained everything to me. He said something like this: "You are now oversensitive to mold. When you get a whiff of mold, your body tries to attack it with antibodies like an autoimmune disease. These antibodies end up attacking all your vital organs—lungs (hence, the chronic cough), liver (hence, the increased liver enzymes in your blood), kidneys, heart (hence, your pulse being very weak), brain (hence, the burning in your brain). That isn't from the brain cells dying. They die a painless death. It is your brain actually trying to heal itself by creating new neural networks, therefore causing all this pain, like an electric current going through your brain. The antibodies live about thirty days in your body, so with even one brief exposure, just a whiff, you're sick for a month. The bad news is that I can't help you. There is no cure. You just have to get away from it. You need to move to the desert."

I asked if I would get over this with time. He said no.

I struggled with all this loss in my life. I had worked hard all my life, and now I had nothing. I had lost it all. I used what little energy, time, and money I had to try to recapture my life as I knew it. I was still striving, but I was so sick, so weak that I could accomplish nothing. I had lost everything.

RETURNING TO THE LORD

At the very beginning of my illness, one of my employees asked me, "Do you believe in yin and yang? You know, that a good thing happens for every bad thing, that there is balance in the universe?"

I was surprised by my response. It came straight from my heart. I said, "No, I believe that is Eastern religious nonsense"

She then asked, "What do you believe?"

I told her, "I believe in good and evil. I believe in God and the Devil and that they do battle for the hearts and souls of men." Then I recited the Apostles' Creed.

> I believe in God the Father Almighty,
> maker of heaven and earth;
> And in Jesus Christ his only Son our Lord:
> who was conceived by the Holy Spirit,
> born of the Virgin Mary,
> suffered under Pontius Pilate,
> was crucified, dead, and buried,
> the third day he rose from the dead;
> he ascended into heaven,
> and sitteth at the right hand of God the Father Almighty;
> from thence he shall come to judge the quick and the dead.
> I believe in the Holy Spirit,

the holy catholic church,
the communion of saints,
the forgiveness of sins,
the resurrection of the body,
and the life everlasting. Amen.

I told her, "That is what I believe." She wasn't expecting that! It was good for her to hear it, and it was very good for me to hear. It was important for me to remind myself of what I really believe. Then and there I knew I had to do something about it. I needed to return to the Lord.

I knew that all of this terrible stuff happened to me for a reason—to bring me back to God. I was being chastened. Some Christians think that God does not punish people, that He is not so cruel as to cause bad things to happen in our lives, but that is simply not true. He says that He does it and that He does it for our own good because He loves us. In Deuteronomy 8:5, He says, "You should know in your heart that as a man chastens his son, so the LORD your God chastens you." This theme is repeated in Proverbs 3:12, "For whom the LORD loves He corrects, Just as a father the son in whom he delights," and in Hebrews 12:5–8, it says,

> And you have forgotten the exhortation which speaks to you as to sons: "My son, do not despise the chastening of the LORD, Nor be discouraged when you are rebuked by Him; For whom the LORD loves He chastens, And scourges every son whom He receives." If you endure chastening, God deals with you as with sons; for what son is there whom a father does not chasten? But if you are without chastening, of which all have become partakers, then you are illegitimate and not sons.

Yes, that's what was happening to me, and ultimately it was a very good thing; however, it took me a long time to realize it, and it hurt!

Later my mom pointed out a Scripture in the book of Haggai that applied specifically to me and my situation. In this book of the Bible God is angry with the people because they ignored Him and His temple and instead concentrated on themselves, their own lives, and their own houses, letting God's temple fall into ruin. Here's what God said in Haggai 1:4–11:

> "Is it time for you yourselves to dwell in your paneled houses, and this temple to lie in ruins?" Now therefore, thus says the Lord of hosts: "Consider your ways! You have sown much, and bring in little; You eat, but do not have enough; You drink, but you are not filled with drink;
>
> You clothe yourselves, but no one is warm; And he who earns wages, earns wages to put into a bag with holes. ... You looked for much, but indeed it came to little; and when you brought it home, I blew it away. Why?" says the Lord of hosts. "Because of My house that is in ruins, while every one of you runs to his own house. Therefore the heavens above you withhold the dew, and the earth withholds its fruit. For I called for a drought on the land and the mountains, on the grain and the new wine and the oil, on whatever the ground brings forth, on men and livestock, and on all the labor of your hands."

Yes, this was very true of me. I worked very hard, and yet it all came to nothing. God blew it away! There was a dark cloud over me. If you are not right with God, He may choose to blow it all away to get your attention, or He may get your attention some other way. Later in Haggai 2:17, applying even more specifically to me, He said, "I struck you with blight and *mildew* and hail in all the labors of your hands; yet you did not turn to Me, says the LORD."

Well, there was no hail, but there was lots of mildew! I realized that I needed to turn to God, that none of this would end as long as I was striving to do it all on my own. The chastening would not end until I had learned my lesson, and I would not be blessed.

It is a sad fact that most of us forget about God when life is good, when things are all going well. When we are successful, smart, hardworking, friendly, wealthy, popular, etc., we often become proud and believe it's all our own doing. We forget that all of that is a gift of God. God warned us about this in Deuteronomy 8:11–20.

> Beware that you do not forget the LORD your God by not keeping His commandments, His judgments, and His statutes which I command you today, lest—when you have eaten and are full, and have built beautiful houses and dwell in them; and when your herds and your flocks multiply, and your silver and your gold are multiplied, and all that you have is multiplied; when your heart is lifted up, and you forget the LORD your God ... then you say in your heart, "My power and the might of my hand have gained me this wealth." And you shall remember the LORD your God, for it is He who gives you power to get wealth, that He may establish His covenant which He swore to your fathers, as it is this day. Then it shall be, if you by any means forget the LORD your God, and follow other gods, and serve them and worship them, I testify against you this day that you shall surely perish. As the nations

which the LORD destroys before you, so you shall perish, because you would not be obedient to the voice of the LORD your God.

If you forget that all your wealth is a blessing from God and if you think that it is all because of your strength, fortitude, intellect, and hard work or that your good looks and charming personality come from Him, then you are in big trouble. In fact, in Deuteronomy 8:20, God said "...so you shall perish because you would not be obedient to the voice of the Lord your God." In these situations it often takes a crisis to bring us back to God, to wake us up. Yes, I was being chastened, and the pain, literal pain, was not going to end until I realized the error of my ways, repented, and returned to God.

What exactly was the error of my ways? After all, I was not a bad guy, I was a good guy. The error of my ways was that I was not obeying the first and greatest commandment. When asked, "What is the greatest commandment?" In Matthew 22:37-38 Jesus answered, "You shall love the LORD your God with all your heart, with all your soul, and with all your mind. This is the first and great commandment." No, I was not doing that. I was not putting God first in my life, and that is what He wants and expects from us. My point is that if you are being chastened by God, the suffering absolutely will not end until you give up all your pride, lay everything at God's feet, and surrender your life to Him. That is the only way. So in my desperation I turned (returned) to the Lord.

I had felt like Job, so I read the book of Job, and yes, my circumstances were pretty much just like his. The difference was that he was more righteous than I, and he had shown much more faith than I did through all his trials. Job had lost everything too—health, home, livestock, possessions, children, etc., and yet he had stayed strong in his faith in God. Job is known for his patience, but it was actually his steadfast and enduring faith in God that pulled him through his trials. In the end he was stronger for it, and the Lord blessed him doubly.

During his trials Job worshipped God and said, "The LORD gave, and the LORD has taken away; Blessed be the name of the LORD." (Job 1:21) So even though God had allowed all these tragedies to befall him, Job was still blessing the name of the Lord. Job also said, "Though He slay me, yet will I trust Him." (Job 13:15) I knew that this is what I needed to do. I had been feeling sorry for myself and trying to carry on when what I should have been doing all along was turning to God as Job did. So I began to follow Job's example.

I spent a lot of time in prayer, reading my Bible and going to church. I read some very good things.

For example, I read James 1:2–5, which says,

> My brethren, count it all joy when you fall into various trials, knowing that the testing of your faith produces patience. But let patience have its perfect work, that you may be perfect and complete, lacking nothing. If any of you lacks wisdom, let him ask of God, who gives to all liberally and without reproach, and it will be given to him.

Count it all joy? Really? You've got to be joking. No, he wasn't joking. He was right!

Similarly when the apostle Paul was suffering, he called on God three times to relieve him, and Paul wrote in 2 Corinthians 12:9 that God did not relieve his suffering but rather He said, "My grace is sufficient for you, for My strength is made perfect in weakness." So I was reminded that God's grace is sufficient for me, and I started to realize that God had allowed all of this to happen to me so that I would come back to Him, forcing me to rely on Him and His grace to strengthen my faith in Him and help me realize that I may live my life according to His will and that He may bless me.

As I was having this epiphany, I remembered something that my mom had said to me when I was a teenager. She said "Read Matthew to live your life. Read John to save your soul." That turned out to be the best advice I ever got!

I read them three times each with a highlighter. Mom was right! In the book of Matthew, Jesus really does tell us how to live our lives, and in the book of John, He tells us how to save our souls. I had read or heard all of these Scriptures before, but it was much more powerful to read them straight through, in their entirety and in this context. As I started talking to other people, sharing this with them, I was amazed to find that so few people knew what Jesus had said. I talked to people in bars, in restaurants, in hotels, at work, at church, among friends, etc. Many had vague or even made-up ideas of what He said, but most people simply didn't know. Even many church people didn't seem to know or didn't remember what Jesus had said. I felt that God was telling me to write this book, to tell everyone what Jesus said about those two subjects—how to live your life and how to save your soul. I have organized it by topic. It is pure truth!

Note that I made a concerted effort not to interpret the Scripture but instead to just present what Jesus said about each topic. I think that you will find Jesus' statements so clear that they do not need interpretation and so powerful that you will want to read the Bible yourself. He says what he means, and means what he says.

CHAPTER 2

Read Matthew to Live Your Life

But seek first the kingdom of God and His righteousness,
and all these things shall be added to you.
—MATTHEW 6:33

WHO IS JESUS?

The book of Matthew is primarily Jesus teaching us how to live our lives, how to relate to God and to one another, and what He expects of us. The book of John, discussed in chapter 3, tells us who Jesus is and why He came. However, Jesus also tells us who He is in the book of Matthew, so let's not look at what other people have said, let's look at what God said, and what Jesus Himself said about who He is:

What God said about Jesus

In Matthew 3:16–17, Jesus was baptized by John the Baptist.,

> When He had been baptized, Jesus came up immediately from the water; and behold, the

heavens were opened to Him, and He saw the Spirit of God descending like a dove and alighting upon Him. And suddenly a voice came from heaven, saying, "This is My beloved Son, in whom I am well pleased."

Then in Matthew 17:5, Jesus took Peter, John, and James up onto a mountain. "While he was still speaking, behold, a bright cloud overshadowed them; and suddenly a voice came out of the cloud, saying, 'This is My beloved Son, in whom I am well pleased. Hear Him!'"

God tells us to listen to Jesus, so let's listen to what Jesus had to say.

What Jesus said about Himself

Jesus tells Peter that He is the Christ.

In Matthew 16:15-17,

> He said to them, *"But who do you say that I am?"* Simon Peter answered and said, "You are the Christ, the Son of the living God." Jesus answered and said to him, *"Blessed are you, Simon Bar-Jonah, for flesh and blood has not revealed this to you, but My Father who is in heaven."*

Then Jesus tells the high priest that He is the Christ.

Matthew 26: 63–64 says,

> And the high priest answered and said to Him, "I put You under oath by the living God: Tell us

if You are the Christ, the Son of God!" Jesus said to him, *"It is as you said. Nevertheless, I say to you, hereafter you will see the Son of Man sitting at the right hand of the Power, and coming on the clouds of heaven."*

The high priest then freaked out and convicted Jesus of blasphemy and then handed Him over to Pilate to be crucified. Read Matthew 27 for details. So we have established that Jesus is the Son of God, the Christ, the Messiah, the Savior.

WHY DID JESUS COME?

To call sinners to repentance

Matthew 9:10–13 says,

> Now it happened, as Jesus sat at the table in the house, that behold, many tax collectors and sinners came and sat down with Him and His disciples. And when the Pharisees saw it, they said to His disciples, "Why does your Teacher eat with tax collectors and sinners?" When Jesus heard that, He said to them, *"Those who are well have no need of a physician, but those who are sick. But go and learn what this means: 'I desire mercy and not sacrifice.' For I did not come to call the righteous, but sinners, to repentance."*

Jesus came to call sinners to repentance. This is something many church people seem to forget. Many Christians only socialize with other Christians. That is terrible. Jesus associated with sinners, and we, too, should love and accept others as He taught us to do.

We should not condone sinful behavior, but we should love the sinner and hate the sin. By the way, when He said He came to call sinners to repentance. That means all of us. Every single one of us is a sinner.

If you don't believe it, if you think you are a good person, just read the Ten Commandments (appendix A). Think about each one. This is God's Law, His standard for righteousness, and there is not one person who has lived up to it. Read them slowly and carefully and think about each one. Have you kept every one of them always? No, of course not. Jesus said, *"No one is good, but One."* By the way, that would be Him. This is why Jesus came—to die for us because we aren't good enough. We can only be saved through Him and by His grace. Jesus tells us this repeatedly in the book of John, which we will see in the next chapter of this book. There is a great book by Andy Stanley about exactly this subject. The book is titled *How Good Is Good Enough.*[3] Also read *God Has a Wonderful Plan for Your Life: The Myth of the Modern Message* by Ray Comfort.[4]

C. S. Lewis states it this way:

> Christianity tells people to repent, and promises them forgiveness. It therefore has nothing to say to people who do not know they have done anything to repent of or who do not feel they need forgiveness. It is after you have realized that there is a Moral Law, and a Power behind the law, and that you have broken the law and put yourself wrong with that Power—it is after all this, and not a moment sooner, that Christianity begins to talk.[5]

Lewis also says, "A moderately bad man knows he is not very good, a thoroughly bad man thinks he is alright."

To give His life a ransom for many

In Matthew 20:26–28 Jesus says,

> *Yet it shall not be so among you; but whoever desires to become great among you, let him be your servant. And whoever desires to be first among you, let him be your slave—just as the Son of Man did not come to be served, but to serve, and to give His life, a ransom for many.*

To save the lost

In Matthew 18:11, He said, *"For the Son of Man has come to save that which was lost."*

So Christ said that we are all sinners, that He calls us to repent of our sins, that He came to give His life to save us by paying our ransom, and that He did it because we are lost. It's pretty clear.

WHAT JESUS SAID...

About God

Seeking Him—Make God your top priority

In Matthew 6:33 Jesus says, *"But seek first the kingdom of God and His righteousness, and all these things shall be added to you."*

Seek Him first, and then He will provide for you! I think this is one of the greatest lessons in the book of Matthew. He tells us to make God our number-one priority. This is a consistent theme with Jesus.

He reminds us of this several times. To put it in context, during this part of the Sermon on the Mount, Jesus is telling us not to worry, that God will provide for us. Matthew 6:25–34 says,

> *Therefore I say to you, do not worry about your life, what you will eat or what you will drink; nor about your body, what you will put on. Is not life more than food and the body more than clothing? Look at the birds of the air, for they neither sow nor reap nor gather into barns; yet your heavenly Father feeds them. Are you not of more value than they? Which of you by worrying can add one cubit to his stature? So why do you worry about clothing? Consider the lilies of the field, how they grow: they neither toil nor spin; and yet I say to you that even Solomon in all his glory was not arrayed like one of these. Now if God so clothes the grass of the field, which today is, and tomorrow is thrown into the oven, will He not much more clothe you, O you of little faith? Therefore do not worry, saying, "What shall we eat?" or "What shall we drink?" or "What shall we wear?" For after all these things the Gentiles seek. For your heavenly Father knows that you need all these things. But seek first the kingdom of God and His righteousness, and all these things shall be added to you. Therefore do not worry about tomorrow, for tomorrow will worry about its own things. Sufficient for the day is its own trouble.*

He tells us not to worry. God will provide for us if we have faith and let Him. There was a great man named R. G. Letourneau, who made Matthew 6:33 his life's verse. He founded one of the most successful heavy-equipment businesses in history, provided 70 percent of the heavy equipment to the US military during WWII, eventually sold his business to Caterpillar, and started a Christian college, a mission in Peru, and a mission in Liberia. His biography is titled *Mover of Men and Mountains.*[6]

Where our treasure lies, there lies our heart. In Matthew 6:19–24 Jesus says,

> *Do not lay up for yourselves treasures on earth, where moth and rust destroy and where thieves break in and steal; but lay up for yourselves treasures in heaven, where neither moth nor rust destroys and where thieves do not break in and steal. For where your treasure is, there your heart will be also … No one can serve two masters; for either he will hate the one and love the other, or else he will be loyal to the one and despise the other. You cannot serve God and mammon.*

He points out that we cannot serve God and riches. It is great to have money, and it's very hard to get by without it; however, our hearts must be for God and for other people, not for money, things, power, fame, popularity, etc. Treasure on earth is fleeting. Treasure in heaven is everlasting, literally eternal.

He points this out again. Matthew 19:21 says, "Jesus said to him, '*If you want to be perfect, go, sell what you have and give to the poor, and you will have treasure in heaven; and come, follow Me.*'"

Jesus isn't telling everyone to go sell and give away everything they have. He was telling this young man to do so because he loved his money more than he loved God, more than he loved other people too. If you love your money too much, God may tell you to do that. If you love God and use your money for His purposes, then He will give you the ability to make more.

So we must treasure God first, other people second, and then all the other things in our lives. This comes through loud and clear in Matthew 22, His greatest commandment, our greatest priority. Matthew 22:37–40 says,

> Jesus said to him, *"You shall love the* LORD *your God with all your heart, with all your soul, and with all your mind." This is the first and great commandment. And the second is like it: "You shall love your neighbor as yourself." On these two commandments hang all the Law and the Prophets.*

This is powerful! How many people do you know who really love God with all their heart and soul and mind? How many people make God their top priority? And how many truly love their neighbors as themselves? We are to love our neighbors as much as we love ourselves, no less. We are commanded to do these two things. They are not optional. Francis Chan wrote a fantastic book about these two commandments titled *Crazy Love*[7] and tells us that Jesus really meant exactly what He said and then tells us how to apply these principles in our lives. There is another book titled *Radical* by David Platt,[8] which is also based on these commandments and points out that the modern church has become too comfortable and too self-serving. By Jesus' example, he shows how to live as Christians, truly loving the Lord and truly loving and helping our neighbors. Awesome stuff!

Listening to God—Hearing His Word

We need the Word of God to live. The first real lesson I learned from Jesus in the book of Matthew came in chapter 4 when He was tempted by Satan in the desert. Jesus was hungry. He had been in the desert for forty days, so the Devil said, "If you are the Son of

God, command that these stones become bread." Jesus replied, *"It is written, 'Man shall not live by bread alone, but by every word that proceeds from the mouth of God'"* (Matthew 4:4).

This is very important. Jesus said that we need the Word of God to live. It's true. It is spiritual food that we need to nourish our souls. I have found that I can't really know God if I don't know what He said. I need to read His Word and to listen to it preached to really know and to understand God and to have a relationship with Him. I find that if I skip it for even a day or two, I start unknowingly drifting away from God. It is so easy to lose focus. Reading the Word keeps me on track, keeps me walking with Him, and keeps God as my top priority.

It may seem awkward to you, and you may not know where to start, so I recommend what my mom recommended, "Read Matthew to live your life. Read John to save your soul." I will add that you should do so slowly and carefully with a highlighter and reread these books throughout your life. Also read Psalms and Proverbs. There is real wisdom here.

I will also add that this is serious business. You can't just read the Bible casually and expect to get anything from it. A friend once told me, "The Bible doesn't really speak to me." Well, you have to be very serious about it. A. W. Tozer said "And the Bible itself, though it is nourishment, though it is light, though it is warmth, though it is medicine to the soul, yet it never helps anybody where there is not serious attention given to it."

C. S. Lewis said, "Consequently, if you do not listen to theology, that will not mean that you have no ideas about God. It will mean that you have a lot of wrong ones." (Lewis, 1952) I find this to be very true. I talk to people who have all kinds of ideas about God, but they have no foundation. They simply make up their own ideas, creating in their minds a god who is what they want him to be.

Hearing the Word of God preached is equally important, so it is important to find a good church. In Romans 10:14–17, the apostle Paul states,

> How then shall they call on Him in whom they have not believed? And how shall they believe in Him of whom they have not heard? And how shall they hear without a preacher? And how shall they preach unless they are sent? … So then faith comes by hearing, and hearing by the word of God.

Choosing a church is difficult because there are so many options—some good, some bad, some very bad. How does one choose? Well, I can recommend a few very good ones that really preach the Word of God, not all kinds of interpretations of it but the actual Word of God. My favorite pastor is Dr. Charles Stanley of In Touch Ministries (www.intouch.org). He is a wise grandfatherly Baptist preacher from Atlanta with real godly wisdom. He is not a jump-up-and-down, holy-roller. He just tells it like it is. I watch his sermons every Sunday morning while I get ready for church. His sermons make a huge difference in my life. I like some of our local preachers here in Ocala, Florida—Tim Gilligan of Meadowbrook Church (www.mbcocala.com) as well as Mickey Graves of Cross Pointe Church (www.crosspointeocala.org). Dr. David Jeremiah of Turning Points Ministries (www.DavidJeremiah.org) in San Diego is also very good. The Calvary Chapel guys are good too—Greg Laurie, Chuck Smith, and Alistair Begg. Justin Miller in Orlando is a fantastic young preacher (getreallife.com), and I think young people will really understand the way this guy relates God's Word to real life. For the intellectual, listen to Ravi Zacharias (www.rzim.org). There are many other good churches as well, but these are my favorites. I trust them to have the knowledge of the Lord and to get it right. I also think it is very important to worship in a church. I know there are all kinds of problems with churches, and many people have left the Church as a result of hypocrisy, self-righteousness, corruption, abuses, etc. That is understandable, but sadly they usually end up drifting away from God as a result of leaving. Once you leave the church, you gradually drift away from God.

In regard to listening to God, there is a good book by Charles Stanley titled *How to Listen to God*.[9] God speaks to us through His written Word, and He also speaks to us through others, through circumstances, and directly. Stanley tells you how to listen. Sometimes when I tell people that God talks to me, they think I'm a freak, but listen to what Stanley says about it. "Jesus made it clear in John 10:27 that the believer's normal experience is to hear God accurately. *'My sheep hear my voice, and I know them, and they follow Me.'*" Stanley also says, "The Holy Spirit living within us and speaking to us ought to be the natural normal lifestyle of believers. We can claim His presence, direction and guidance."

I have had people ask me, "Why doesn't God speak to me?" Charles Stanley says,

> The only message that an unbeliever will ever hear from God is that he is a sinner who needs to look to Jesus as his Savior. Until that person knows Christ as his personal Messiah, he will not hear God speak on any subject other than salvation. (C. Stanley, 1985)

Although people don't like to hear that, it was certainly true in my own life. When I was fourteen years old, the only thing I heard from God was that I was a sinner and needed to be saved. I was guilty and convicted by the Holy Spirit. I sat in the pews at church and squirmed. I knew I needed Christ, but I did not want Christ. I was a happy, smart kid with a strong will, a strong mind, and a strong body. I had everything going for me, and I didn't want to submit my will to God. Frankly that sounded absolutely crazy to me. I wanted to do whatever I wanted to do. I was doing just fine. Finally I did accept Christ as my Savior (details to come in Chapter 3). Then God could talk to me, not before. You see, when we are going against God's will, we are separated from God, and He won't hear us, and won't talk to us.

Isaiah 59:2 says, "But your iniquities have separated you from your God; And your sins have hidden His face from you, So that He will not hear."

Once you are born again, redeemed by Jesus Christ, your sins are washed away. You are forgiven. God can hear you, listen to you, and speak to you then, but not before.

Praying

Jesus taught us how to pray in Matthew 6:8–15, which says,

> *And when you pray, you shall not be like the hypocrites. For they love to pray standing in the synagogues and on the corners of the streets, that they may be seen by men. Assuredly, I say to you, they have their reward. But you, when you pray, go into your room, and when you have shut your door, pray to your Father who is in the secret place; and your Father who sees in secret will reward you openly. And when you pray, do not use vain repetitions as the heathen do. For they think that they will be heard for their many words. Therefore do not be like them. For your Father knows the things you have need of before you ask Him. In this manner, therefore, pray:*

Our Father in heaven,
Hallowed be Your name.
Your kingdom come.
Your will be done
On earth as it is in heaven.
Give us this day our daily bread.
And forgive us our debts,
As we forgive our debtors.
And do not lead us into temptation,
But deliver us from the evil one.
For Thine is the kingdom and the power and
the glory forever.
Amen.

I pray this prayer every morning to start off my day. I pray for other things too, but I pray the Lord's Prayer first, as this is what Jesus taught us to do. There is a danger that it becomes ritualistic, that we just recite it. Don't recite it, pray it. Actually think about it as you are praying it and pray it with sincerity. It is powerful when you do that. You don't have to ask Him for all the details. Jesus is clear on this. He says God knows what we need before we ask, so we should ask for His will to be done in our lives.

I then pray the Prayer of Jabez in 1 Chronicles 4:10. "Oh, that You would bless me indeed, and enlarge my territory, that Your hand would be with me, and that You would keep me from evil, that I may not cause pain!"

After that I ask for God's forgiveness. I thank Him for my many blessings and ask for His guidance, wisdom, strength, and courage. Then I pray for my kids, family, friends, company, our country, etc., but I always pray the Lord's Prayer first, asking that His will be done.

Daily prayer has become a very important part of my life. It helps me, and my prayers help others. God hears our prayers. James 5:16 says, "The effectual fervent prayers of a righteous man avails much." When I make time to pray and read God's Word every morning, then He walks with me throughout the day. When I skip it, even for a day or two, I notice a negative difference in my life. I've read that throughout his life, George Washington rose early, read the Bible, and prayed every morning for half an hour. I've had people tell me they don't have time for that. That is the stupidest thing I have ever heard (and I used to think that way myself). I don't have time for God? Make time. It is the most important thing you can do in your life.

Charles Stanley says, "When we tell God we don't have time for Him, we are really saying we don't have time for life, for joy, for direction, or for prosperity, because He is the source of all these." (C. Stanley, 1985)

Now I want to make something very clear. When I talk about prayer, this is not some meditation that gives me inner peace or self-awareness. This is not something to relax me and clear my mind. This is not getting in touch with the energy of the universe. It is none of that New Age spiritual, psychological stuff. This is talking to God and listening to God. It is a real relationship. He is real.

Ask Him, seek Him, and knock on His door. In Matthew 7:7–8 Jesus says, *"Ask, and it will be given to you; seek, and you will find; knock, and it will be opened to you. 8 For everyone who asks receives, and he who seeks finds, and to him who knocks it will be opened."*

So Jesus tells us to keep asking God, keep seeking Him, and keep knocking at His door. He will answer. It may not seem like it. It may take longer than you would like, but He will. He may not answer the way we want Him to and usually not when and how we expect Him to, but He will answer. It may take months. It may take years, but don't give up. God's timing isn't the same as our timing, and His way isn't the same as our way. It is better. So we must have faith, and keep asking, keep seeking, and keep knocking. When you do this consistently and persistently, you will grow in your relationship with God, and it will change your life.

Good Works

Do good to please God, not to make yourself look good or feel good. In Matthew 6:1–4 Jesus says,

> *Take heed that you do not do your charitable deeds before men, to be seen by them. Otherwise you have no reward from your Father in heaven. Therefore, when you do a charitable deed, do not sound a trumpet before you as the hypocrites do in the synagogues and in the streets, that they may have glory from men. Assuredly, I say to you, they have their reward. But when you do a charitable deed, do not let your left hand know what your right hand is doing, that your charitable deed may be in secret; and your Father who sees in secret will Himself reward you openly.*

So when you make a donation to a hospital, a university, or a church, don't insist they name the building after you. Just do it and don't tell anyone you did it. Or if you feed the poor, don't brag about it, just do it. God will know. He's the only one that matters.

Faith in God—Having it and Sharing it

Jesus told us to have faith. Faith can move mountains. Matthew 17:20 says, *"For assuredly, I say to you, if you have faith as a mustard seed, you will say to this mountain, 'Move from here to there,' and it will move; and nothing will be impossible for you."*

And in Matthew 18:19–20 He says, *"Again I say to you that if two of you agree on earth concerning anything that they ask, it will be done for them by My Father in heaven. For where two or three are gathered together in My name, I am there in the midst of them."*

There is a very important principle here. Jesus says if two or three agree, it will be done for them by the Father. He wants us to pray together in His name, and our prayers are powerful when prayed together that way.

The centurion had real faith. This has always been one of my favorite stories in the Bible, showing the power of strong faith. Matthew 8:5–10 says,

> Now when Jesus had entered Capernaum, a centurion came to Him, pleading with Him, saying, "Lord, my servant is lying at home paralyzed, dreadfully tormented." And Jesus said to him, *"I will come and heal him."* The centurion answered and said, "Lord, I am not worthy that You should come under my roof. But only speak a word, and my servant will be healed. For I also am a man under authority, having soldiers under me. And I say to this one, 'Go,' and he goes; and to another, 'Come,' and he comes; and to my servant, 'Do this,' and he does it." When Jesus heard it, He marveled, and said to those who followed, *"Assuredly, I say to you, I have not found such great faith, not even in Israel!"* ... Then Jesus said to the centurion, *"Go your way; and as you have believed, so let it be done for you."* And his servant was healed that same hour.

Keep your eyes on Jesus, and you can walk on water. Matthew 14:29–31 says,

> So He said, *"Come."* And when Peter had come down out of the boat, he walked on the water to go to Jesus. But when he saw that the wind was boisterous, he was afraid; and beginning to sink he cried out, saying, "Lord, save me!" And immediately Jesus stretched out His hand and caught him, and said to him, *"O you of little faith, why did you doubt?"*

The lesson here is that as long as Peter kept his eyes on Christ, he had enough faith to walk on water! He could do anything. As soon as he took his eyes off of Christ and focused on the wind and the waves, all of the troubles in life, then he lost faith and started to sink. Keep your eyes on the Lord! As the apostle Paul said to the Philippians 4:13, "I can do all things in Christ who strengthens me."

Jesus told us to share our faith! Confess Jesus Christ before men. In Matthew 10:32–33 He says, *"Therefore whoever confesses Me before men, him I will also confess before My Father who is in heaven. But whoever denies Me before men, him I will also deny before My Father who is in heaven."*

These are the words of Jesus Christ. He says we must confess to other people that we are Christians, that Jesus Christ is our Lord and Savior. Don't hide it. He's says that if we don't do it, He will deny us before the Father. Imagine that you are hanging out with some friends and one of them says, "Oh, yeah, I'm getting more spiritual. I'm meditating and becoming one with the universe," or that person could say, "I'm thinking of becoming Buddhist." Then you say something really stupid like, "That's cool." You just blew it! As a Christian, you have not only an opportunity but also an obligation to share your faith in Christ at that moment. If you don't, then Jesus says he will deny you before the Father. Now imagine that you die and you face God on judgment day, and Jesus says, "I never knew you, depart from me" (Matthew 7:23). That's not good, but that is exactly what He says He will do if we deny Him before men.

In today's culture it has become increasingly popular to deny Him, to just not talk about it. It is not politically correct. People don't want to hear it. I have been told, "It is private," or, "My faith is a personal thing between me and God." Yes, it is, but Jesus commands us to share it. He does not make that optional. I have been told that I shouldn't talk about Christ because it is disrespectful to people of other faiths. I say, "So what? Jesus told me to do it. I'm going to do it." It may be unpopular. It may make me unpopular, but it is the right thing to do. Jesus not only tells us to confess Him before men, but He goes on to tell us that if we don't, then He will not confess us before the Father. That cannot go well for us! We shouldn't worry about what others think. We shouldn't even mind if we are persecuted for our faith. In a few places in the book of Matthew, Jesus tells us that we will suffer persecution in His name.

I also think this is very important for our country. In the past, most of our Founding Fathers and most of our presidents and other leaders would actively declare Christ before the entire nation in their prayers and proclamations. Nowadays that is considered political suicide. I think it is spiritual suicide for our nation if we don't do it. Psalm 33:12 says, "Blessed is the nation who's god is the Lord." I believe the opposite is true as well. Who do you fear? God or man?

Matthew 10:27 says, *"Whatever I tell you in the dark, speak in the light; and what you hear in the ear, preach on the housetops."* And then in Matthew 11:6 Jesus says, *"And blessed is he who is not offended because of Me."*

Jesus Christ exposes our sin, points out our inadequacy before almighty God, shows us our need for forgiveness and for salvation, and tells us we must come to Him. We must surrender our will to Him, surrender our lives to Him. Many people are very offended by that message. He tells us not to be one of those people.

In Matthew 5:14–16 Jesus says, *"You are the light of the world. A city that is set on a hill cannot be hidden. Nor do they light a lamp and put it under a basket, but on a lampstand, and it gives light to all who are in the house. Let your light so shine before men, that they may see your good works and glorify your Father in heaven."*

We are to glorify the Father. We can't do that if we hide our faith. We can't do that if we keep it under a basket. This almost seems to contradict Matthew 6:1, where Jesus tells us not to do charitable deeds before men to be seen by them, but what He is saying is that we shouldn't do good works for our own glory. We should do good works for God's glory.

Finally Jesus gave us the Great Commission in Matthew 28:18–20. After Jesus rose from the dead, He met the disciples in Galilee and gave them the Great Commission.

And Jesus came and spoke to them, saying, *"All authority has been given to Me in heaven and on earth. Go therefore and make disciples of all the nations, baptizing them in the name of the Father and of the Son and of the Holy Spirit, teaching them to observe all things that I have commanded you; and lo, I am with you always, even to the end of the age."* Amen.

Jesus said this to the eleven disciples, but it applies to all Christians. After all, that is the definition of a Christian, a disciple of Jesus Christ. I've even heard preachers say something like, "Stop looking for God's will for your life. He already told you what to do. He gave us the Great Commission, so just go and do it!" Good advice.

Peace and Rest

In Matthew 11:28–30 He says,

> *Come to Me, all you who labor and are heavy laden,*
> *and I will give you rest. Take My yoke upon you and*
> *learn from Me, for I am gentle and lowly in heart, and*
> *you will find rest for your souls. For My yoke is easy*
> *and My burden is light.*

This does not mean that you will not be tired and weary. It does not mean that you will not have troubles and trials. What He means is that you can lay those cares on Him and trust in Him. He will give you peace in your soul if you will accept it. It's true! As the apostle Paul said in Philippians 4:6-7, "Be anxious for nothing, but in everything by prayer and supplication, with thanksgiving, let your requests be made known to God; and the peace of God, which surpasses all understanding, will guard your hearts and minds through Christ Jesus."

By the way, He said, *"Come to me."* You can only get this rest if you come to Him. You can't get it if you do not know Jesus as your Lord and Savior.

Serving God, Following Christ

Matthew 16:24–27 says,

> Then Jesus said to His disciples, *"If anyone desires to*
> *come after Me, let him deny himself, and take up his*
> *cross, and follow Me. For whoever desires to save his*
> *life will lose it, but whoever loses his life for My sake*
> *will find it. For what profit is it to a man if he gains*

*the whole world, and loses his own soul? Or what will
a man give in exchange for his soul? For the Son of
Man will come in the glory of His Father with His
angels, and then He will reward each according to
his works."*

So if you want to save your own life, if you put yourself ahead of
Jesus, you will lose it, but if you put Him first, He will give you life.
He expects us to give up our will and submit to His will, and *then*
we will find life. It may be difficult for all of us independent types,
but this is what He requires of us. It is important to understand that
by giving your life to Christ and submitting your will to His will
as He commands us to do, that does not take away who you are,
but instead allows you to become who you really are and who God
intended you to be. You are still the same person but better.

Jesus tells us not to be self-seeking, *"for what profit is it to a man if
he gains the whole world but loseth his own soul."* Clearly there is no
profit in it! Jesus is telling us to follow Him, or else we will lose our
own souls.

C. S. Lewis talked about this in *Mere Christianity.*

> The Christian way is harder, and easier. Christ says,
> "Give me All. I don't want so much of your time
> and so much of your money and so much of your
> work: I want You. I have not come to torment your
> natural self, but to kill it. No half-measures are any
> good ... Hand over the whole natural self, all the
> desires which you think innocent as well as the ones
> you think wicked—the whole outfit. I will give you
> a new self instead. In fact, I will give you Myself: my
> own will shall become yours." The terrible thing, the
> almost impossible thing, is to hand over your whole

self—all your wishes and precautions—to Christ. But it is far easier than what we are all trying to do instead. For what we are trying to do is to remain what we call "ourselves," to keep personal happiness as our great aim in life, and yet at the same time be "good." We are all trying to let our mind and heart go their own way—centered on money or pleasure or ambition—and hoping, in spite of this, to behave honestly and chastely and humbly. And that is exactly what Christ warned us you could not do.

Jesus demands complete dedication to Him. In Matthew 10:34–39 He says,

> *Do not think that I came to bring peace on earth. I did not come to bring peace but a sword. For I have come to "set a man against his father, a daughter against her mother, and a daughter-in-law against her mother-in-law"; and "a man's enemies will be those of his own household." He who loves father or mother more than Me is not worthy of Me. And he who loves son or daughter more than Me is not worthy of Me. And he who does not take his cross and follow after Me is not worthy of Me. He who finds his life will lose it, and he who loses his life for My sake will find it.*

Huh? I thought he was bringing "peace on earth, good will toward men." This one is very hard for us. We all love our families and friends, and if our families and friends are nonbelievers and if they mock us for believing in Christ, this can cause a lot of strife. Some will believe, and some won't. This division does tear apart relationships, friendships, and even families, but this is the devotion that Jesus demands of us, to give up our lives for Him, and in return, He will give us eternal life. Tough stuff, but it's true, and it's worth it.

You are either with Him or against Him. Matthew 12:30 says, "Jesus said, *'He who is not with Me is against Me, and he who does not gather with Me scatters abroad.'*"

Jesus says that we can't be neutral, that if we are not working for Him, we are working against Him. You simply cannot deny Christ as Lord and get away with it. It can't happen. There are only two sides—God and Satan. If you are not with Christ, you are with Satan. For example, if you are trying to do good works to help your fellow man and you are not believing in and trusting in Christ, then you are against Him, and as He states, you "*scatter abroad.*" What you are doing is trying to do good in your own strength, in your own power, out of your own goodness, and in doing so, you are a bad example to others. Jesus tells us we can do nothing without Him. People really hate hearing this, but He's the one who said it, not me. I just happen to believe Him.

Followers of Jesus will be rewarded. In Matthew 19:29–30 He says, *"And everyone who has left houses or brothers or sisters or father or mother or wife or children or lands, for My name's sake, shall receive a hundredfold, and inherit eternal life. But many who are first will be last, and the last first."*

Put Christ first in your life, and you will be rewarded for it in heaven.

What Jesus said about how we treat other people

Forgiveness

In Matthew 6:14–15 Jesus says, *"For if you forgive men their trespasses, your heavenly Father will also forgive you. But if you do not forgive men their trespasses, neither will your Father forgive your trespasses."*

This is serious stuff. He is telling us that we must forgive *everyone* who has wronged us, no carrying grudges. If we keep grudges, He will not forgive us. He did not say that we should forgive them if they ask. He did not say that we should forgive them if they deserve it. He said that we should forgive them, period. We must forgive everyone who has wronged us—brothers, sisters, children, parents, friends, colleagues, ex-spouses, strangers, etc., no matter the offense.

I do not think Jesus made that statement lightly. We need His forgiveness. It is the entire reason Christ came, as we will discuss when we get to John 3. So we must forgive everyone who has wronged us. He is not giving us a choice. We must forgive them, or we will not be forgiven. And if we are not forgiven, we will burn in hell.

Forgiveness Again

Matthew 18:21–22 says, "Then Peter came to Him and said, 'Lord, how often shall my brother sin against me, and I forgive him? Up to seven times?' Jesus said to him, *'I do not say to you, up to seven times, but up to seventy times seven.'*" Then in Matthew 18:23–35, Jesus tells a parable of a servant who owed his master money and begged forgiveness. The master forgave the debt, but then the servant found a man who owed him and demanded payment, threatened him, and then threw him into debtor's prison. When the master found out that his servant would not forgive his debtors as he had been forgiven, here's what Jesus said happened:

> *And his master was angry, and delivered him to the torturers until he should pay all that was due to him. "So My heavenly Father also will do to you if each of you, from his heart, does not forgive his brother his trespasses."*

So Jesus said that if we don't forgive others, God will deliver us to the torturers. That sounds very bad!

Do Not Judge!

In Matthew 7:1, Jesus said, *"Judge not that you may not be judged."* I personally think that many Christians forget this one altogether. They often judge others. They will see other people who are sinners and somehow forget that they too are sinners, and rather than loving them as Jesus did, they judge them. This is really terrible, and Jesus said that it was terrible in Matthew 7:2–5.

> *For with what judgment you judge, you will be judged; and with the measure you use, it will be measured back to you. And why do you look at the speck in your brother's eye, but do not consider the plank in your own eye? Or how can you say to your brother, "Let me remove the speck from your eye"; and look, a plank is in your own eye? Hypocrite! First remove the plank from your own eye, and then you will see clearly to remove the speck from your brother's eye.*

Did you notice how stern He is here? If we judge others, we will be judged by the same measure. Yes, Jesus is one serious dude. Once again He says what He means, and He means what He says.

Helping Others

Jesus tells us to help our brother in need or burn in hell. It's our choice. In Matthew 25:31–46 Jesus says,

> *When the Son of Man comes in His glory, and all the holy angels with Him, then He will sit on the throne of His glory. All the nations will be gathered before Him, and He will separate them one from another, as a shepherd divides his sheep from the goats. And He will*

set the sheep on His right hand, but the goats on the left. Then the King will say to those on His right hand, "Come, you blessed of My Father, inherit the kingdom prepared for you from the foundation of the world: for I was hungry and you gave Me food; I was thirsty and you gave Me drink; I was a stranger and you took Me in; I was naked and you clothed Me; I was sick and you visited Me; I was in prison and you came to Me." Then the righteous will answer Him, saying, "Lord, when did we see You hungry and feed You, or thirsty and give You drink? When did we see You a stranger and take You in, or naked and clothe You? Or when did we see You sick, or in prison, and come to You?" And the King will answer and say to them, "Assuredly, I say to you, inasmuch as you did it to one of the least of these My brethren, you did it to Me." Then He will also say to those on the left hand, "Depart from Me, you cursed, into the everlasting fire prepared for the devil and his angels: for I was hungry and you gave Me no food; I was thirsty and you gave Me no drink; I was a stranger and you did not take Me in, naked and you did not clothe Me, sick and in prison and you did not visit Me." Then they also will answer Him, saying, "Lord, when did we see You hungry or thirsty or a stranger or naked or sick or in prison, and did not minister to You?" Then He will answer them, saying, "Assuredly, I say to you, inasmuch as you did not do it to one of the least of these, you did not do it to Me." And these will go away into everlasting punishment, but the righteous into eternal life.

Jesus tells us to help our brother in need, and He will reward us in heaven. If we ignore our brother in need, we will burn in *"the everlasting fire prepared for the devil and his angels."* He said it, not me!

Love Your Enemies

In Matthew 5:38–42 Jesus says,

> *You have heard that it was said, "An eye for an eye*
> *and a tooth for a tooth." But I tell you not to resist an*
> *evil person. But whoever slaps you on your right cheek,*
> *turn the other to him also. If anyone wants to sue you*
> *and take away your tunic, let him have your cloak also.*
> *And whoever compels you to go one mile, go with him*
> *two. Give to him who asks you, and from him who*
> *wants to borrow from you do not turn away.*

This really flies in the face of our culture, but Jesus is clear about this. He tells us what we should do. If someone is mean to you, be nice to them by showing love, kindness, and forgiveness. If someone sues you and literally tries to take the shirt off your back, don't fight them in court. Give it to them and give them your coat too. Give them more than they ask for, and if someone needs a hand, help them, and if they want to borrow money, give it to them. How many of us really do this? We should. He tells us to do it. He meant it. We are so trained to look out for ourselves, to stand up for ourselves that Jesus' attitude here is very foreign to us, but He is right. He is God. (We'll talk about that in the next chapter.)

In Matthew 5:43–48 Jesus has more to say about loving our enemies.

> *You have heard that it was said, "You shall love your*
> *neighbor and hate your enemy." But I say to you, love*
> *your enemies, bless those who curse you, do good to*
> *those who hate you, and pray for those who spitefully*
> *use you and persecute you, that you may be sons of your*
> *Father in heaven; for He makes His sun rise on the evil*
> *and on the good, and sends rain on the just and on the*

unjust. For if you love those who love you, what reward have you? Do not even the tax collectors do the same? And if you greet your brethren only, what do you do more than others? Do not even the tax collectors do so? Therefore you shall be perfect, just as your Father in heaven is perfect.

So Jesus tells us to love everyone, even our enemies, even bad people, and he says that if we do, then we may be sons of the Father in heaven. He's saying that if we don't love them, then we are not sons of the Father. That's pretty bad. He also said *"He makes the sun rise on the evil and the good."* Jesus tells us a few times not to hate evil people and not to worry about justice and fairness. You see, God has a plan for them too. "God desires all men to be saved and to come to the knowledge of the truth" (1 Timothy 2:4)

Loving Your Neighbor

In the Sermon on the Mount, Jesus gave us the Golden Rule. Matthew 7:12 says, *"Therefore, whatever you want men to do to you, do also to them, for this is the Law and the Prophets."*

This is the Golden Rule, and I see this command being broken all the time by most everyone, even good people. People treat their friends, family, neighbors, coworkers, and others worse than they would want to be treated, and frankly they are often self-righteous about it with an attitude that says, "Well, that's what they deserve." If they treat their friends that way, just imagine how they treat the lowly people—the beggar, the drunkard, the addict, the thief, etc. We are to love them all and treat them all as we would want to be treated.

What is the greatest commandment? Matthew 22:37–40 says,

> Jesus said to him, *"You shall love the* LORD *your God with all your heart, with all your soul, and with all your mind." This is the first and great commandment. And the second is like it: "You shall love your neighbor as yourself." On these two commandments hang all the Law and the Prophets.*

So from these Scriptures it is quite clear that we are to love our neighbors as we love ourselves, no less. Think about that carefully. Think about what it means to truly love your neighbor as much as you love yourself, and once again I encourage you to read Francis Chan's book *Crazy Love*. He really explains what it means to love your neighbor as yourself. This goes right along with Jesus' theme of serving and putting God first, others second, and ourselves last. Also read *Radical* by David Platt, who explains what Jesus meant the church to be as opposed to what it has become.

In Matthew 12:48-50 Jesus says, *"'Who is My mother and who are My brothers?' And He stretched out His hand toward His disciples and said, 'Here are My mother and My brothers! For whoever does the will of My Father in heaven is My brother and sister and mother.'"*

Everyone in the body of Christ is our family. So we should treat them as such, no less than you would treat yourself or your own family. This is pretty hard to do, even when it involves people that we like, much less people that we don't like.

Marriage and Divorce

In Matthew 5:31–32 Jesus says, *"Furthermore it has been said, 'Whoever divorces his wife, let him give her a certificate of divorce.' But I say to you that whoever divorces his wife for any reason except sexual immorality causes her to commit adultery; and whoever marries a woman who is divorced commits adultery."*

Matthew 19:3–9 then says,

> The Pharisees also came to Him, testing Him, and saying to Him, "Is it lawful for a man to divorce his wife for just any reason?" And He answered and said to them, *"Have you not read that He who made them at the beginning made them male and female, and said, 'For this reason a man shall leave his father and mother and be joined to his wife, and the two shall become one flesh' So then, they are no longer two but one flesh. Therefore what God has joined together, let not man separate."* They said to Him, "Why then did Moses command to give a certificate of divorce, and to put her away?" He said to them, *"Moses, because of the hardness of your hearts, permitted you to divorce your wives, but from the beginning it was not so. And I say to you, whoever divorces his wife, except for sexual immorality, and marries another, commits adultery; and whoever marries her who is divorced commits adultery."*

Oops, I personally messed up on this one. I'd better do some serious praying and repenting! I do have five tidbits of practical advice here. First reread 1 Corinthians 13:4-8,

> Love suffers long and is kind; love does not envy; love does not parade itself, is not puffed up; does not behave rudely, does not seek its own, is not provoked, thinks no evil; does not rejoice in iniquity, but rejoices in the truth; bears all things, believes all things, hopes all things, endures all things. Love never fails.

This is commonly recited at weddings, and yet a few years later 50 percent of couples seem to forget this and end up divorced. If every couple would truly live like this, there would be no divorce, no broken homes. I think every couple should post it on their refrigerator and read it and live it every day. I'm serious.

Second, read John Eldredge's book *Wild at Heart*[10] (for men) and the companion book *Captivating*[11] (for women). These are not your average self-help books. They really explain what's in a man's heart and what's in a woman's heart from a Christian perspective— awesome, powerful stuff. They will help couples to truly understand each other, relate to each other, and love each other.

Third and most important of all is to commit the marriage to God daily. In Billy Graham's book *The Journey*,[12] he has a very good discussion about this in chapters 25 and 26. This is a great book about living your life with God and walking with Him on a daily basis.

Fourth, read Ephesians 5:33 and live it. "Nevertheless let each one of you in particular so love his own wife as himself, and let the wife see that she respects her husband."

I heard Greg Laurie of Calvary Chapel in Costa Mesa give a sermon on marriage, and he said that in more than thirty years of ministry he has observed that everyone who follows this Scripture has a good marriage and that everyone who doesn't has a bad marriage. He said that it doesn't mean that if you follow it, you will never disagree, but it does mean that you will have a good, strong marriage. Read the entire passage here:

> Wives, submit to your own husbands, as to the
> Lord. For the husband is head of the wife, as also
> Christ is head of the church; and He is the Savior
> of the body. Therefore, just as the church is subject
> to Christ, so let the wives be to their own husbands

in everything. Husbands, love your wives, just as Christ also loved the church and gave Himself for her, that He might sanctify and cleanse her with the washing of water by the word, that He might present her to Himself a glorious church, not having spot or wrinkle or any such thing, but that she should be holy and without blemish ... Nevertheless let each one of you in particular so love his own wife as himself, and let the wife see that she respects her husband. (Ephesians 5:22–33)

Let me explain what happens if you don't do this. Let's say that the husband is not very loving to his wife. Perhaps he is too wrapped up in his work, too bitter, too angry, too worried, and he takes it out on her. He is hard on her and critical of her, and he forgets to let her know that he loves her and forgets to delight in her. What happens then? She will lose respect for him, and she will get angry, controlling, etc. Or she will withdraw, and she won't be very lovable. Then he will love her less. It is a rapid downward spiral. Likewise, if the wife is disrespectful of her husband, if she is nagging, bossy, controlling, etc., then he will find her unlovable and will give her less love (even though she is doing all that because she wants more love). She then will be less respectful of him, and he will love her less. This downward spiral is very rapid and very dangerous. As soon as a husband is aware that he is treating the wife in an unloving way, he needs to correct it, and as soon as a wife realizes that she is treating her husband in a disrespectful way, she needs to correct that too. If you both insist on blaming the other person, the spiral continues downhill very rapidly, and the marriage fails. I believe that this is a natural and common tendency for most people. God gave us the solution. Husbands, love your wives. Wives, respect your husbands.

Fifth, marry the right person, someone who is of a like mind. God warns us repeatedly in the Old Testament not to marry foreign women. Why? Is He nationalist or racist? No, of course not. He tells us why. It is because they will lead us away from Him because of their religion or lack of it. Also, Paul tells us in 2 Corinthians 6:14, "Be you not unequally yoked together with unbelievers: for what fellowship has righteousness with unrighteousness? and what communion has light with darkness?" I don't think God has a problem with you marrying a foreign Christian. I do think it is important that you both share the same faith. It can tear your marriage apart if you don't.

Children

Matthew 19:13–15 says,

> Then little children were brought to Him that He might put His hands on them and pray, but the disciples rebuked them. But Jesus said, *"Let the little children come to Me, and do not forbid them; for of such is the kingdom of heaven."* And He laid His hands on them and departed from there.

Humble yourself as a little child. Matthew 18:2–5 says,

> At that time the disciples came to Jesus, saying, "Who then is greatest in the kingdom of heaven?" Then Jesus called a little child to Him, set him in the midst of them, and said, *"Assuredly, I say to you, unless you are converted and become as little children, you will by no means enter the kingdom of heaven. Therefore whoever humbles himself as this little child is the greatest in the kingdom of heaven. Whoever receives one little child like this in My name receives Me."*

You must be converted and humble yourself as a little child. Jesus said it. If you want to be the tough guy who is independent of God and go through life on your own without His guidance in your life, you are not going to make it to heaven by being good. Jesus said so. Then He warns us in Matthew 18:6–7,

> *Whoever causes one of these little ones who believe in Me to sin, it would be better for him if a millstone were hung around his neck, and he were drowned in the depth of the sea. Woe to the world because of offenses! For offenses must come, but woe to that man by whom the offense comes!*

Now this is just my opinion, but I don't think Jesus is speaking only of little children but of all of His children, meaning any believer. So if we cause any of His children to sin, woe unto us.

Serving God and Man

Always put others before yourself. In Matthew 20:26–28 Jesus says,

> *Yet it shall not be so among you; but whoever desires to become great among you, let him be your servant. And whoever desires to be first among you, let him be your slave—just as the Son of Man did not come to be served, but to serve, and to give His life a ransom for many.*

By serving our fellow man, we are serving God. It is everyone's duty to serve our fellow man just as Christ came to serve us. Four times in the book of Matthew, Jesus says that the first shall be last and the last shall be first. Don't put yourself ahead of others. We live in a selfish society. We are literally taught to look out for number one. Jesus tells us repeatedly that is wrong. We are to put God first, others second, and ourselves last.

Evil People

Jesus talks about good people and bad people in the parable of the wheat and the tares in Matthew 13:24–30.

The kingdom of heaven is like a man who sowed good seed in his field; but while men slept, his enemy came and sowed tares among the wheat and went his way. But when the grain had sprouted and produced a crop, then the tares also appeared. So the servants of the owner came and said to him, "Sir, did you not sow good seed in your field? How then does it have tares?" He said to them, "An enemy has done this." The servants said to him, "Do you want us then to go and gather them up?" But he said, "No, lest while you gather up the tares you also uproot the wheat with them. Let both grow together until the harvest, and at the time of harvest I will say to the reapers, 'First gather together the tares and bind them in bundles to burn them, but gather the wheat into my barn.'"

Then Jesus explains the parable in Matthew 13:37–43.

He who sows the good seed is the Son of Man. The field is the world, the good seeds are the sons of the kingdom, but the tares are the sons of the wicked one. The enemy who sowed them is the devil, the harvest is the end of the age, and the reapers are the angels. Therefore as the tares are gathered and burned in the fire, so it will be at the end of this age. The Son of Man will send out His angels, and they will gather out of His kingdom all things that offend, and those who practice lawlessness, and will cast them into the furnace of fire. There will be wailing and gnashing of teeth. Then the righteous will shine forth as the sun in the kingdom of their Father. He who has ears to hear, let him hear!

Several times Jesus tells us that we should not worry about evil people and that we should not be concerned or frustrated that evil people prosper alongside the good because that doesn't seem fair to us. He says to leave them alone, or you may uproot the good with the bad. He has a purpose for the bad people too. Perhaps that bad person supports many good people, or perhaps God may use that person to do something extraordinary. He is wiser than us. Let Him deal with it. He assures us that the evil may prosper now; however, in the end they will be cast into the furnace of fire, and there will be wailing and gnashing of teeth. Scary!

What Jesus Said about Ourselves

Build Your Foundation on the Rock

In Matthew 7:24–27 Jesus says,

Therefore whoever hears these sayings of Mine, and does them, I will liken him to a wise man who built his house on the rock: and the rain descended, the floods came, and the winds blew and beat on that house; and it did not fall, for it was founded on the rock. But everyone who hears these sayings of Mine, and does not do them, will be like a foolish man who built his house on the sand: and the rain descended, the floods came,

and the winds blew and beat on that house; and it fell.
And great was its fall.

To put this Scripture in context, this is the closing statement in the Sermon on the Mount. Jesus just spent an entire three chapters in the book of Matthew teaching the people how to live, how to interact with one another, and how to interact with God. So now He is telling them, "If you do what I said, build your house on this rock, then you are wise, your house will be strong, and it will stand. But if you don't, then you are a fool, and when the storms of life come—and they will come—your house will fall, and great will be the fall." It's another stern warning. He's like a loving parent, isn't He? He's telling us we can choose to be wise and follow Him, or we can be fools and go our own way. It's our choice.

This message is very important. It makes me grateful for the solid foundation my mother gave us as children, insisting we all go to church and to Sunday school and church camp—though we didn't want to go—and making sure we said grace at the evening meal and teaching us about faith in God through her strong example. She taught us how to build a strong foundation on the Rock of Jesus Christ. So I encourage all of you who are parents or will be parents to give your children that foundation. Show them by your example.

I meet many young people today in their twenties who do not have that foundation. It is very sad. For some reason their parents didn't give them that foundation, stopped going to church, drifted away from God, and did not make Him a priority for their children. So the kids grew up without this foundation. These are fine young men and women—smart, good-hearted, hardworking—but they lack the foundation on the Rock. As long as their lives are going well, they are happy; however, when the storms come—and they do come—they find they do not have a foundation, and their houses fall. They are lost.

However, it's never too late. If you did not provide your kids with that foundation, do it now. If you are getting old and have children and grandchildren but you didn't give them a solid foundation in Jesus Christ, then do it now. Call them up, ask them to go to church with you, have them over for dinner and pray before the meal, etc. Just do it. It is the greatest gift you can possibly give your children. If you have not built your own house on the Rock of Jesus Christ, do it now.

Proverbs 22:6 says, "Train up a child in the way he should go, And when he is old he will not depart from it."

Deuteronomy 6:5–7 says,

> You shall love the LORD your God with all your heart, with all your soul, and with all your strength. And these words which I command you today shall be in your heart. You shall teach them diligently to your children, and shall talk of them when you sit in your house, when you walk by the way, when you lie down, and when you rise up.

So we should be teaching our children about the Lord God in everything we do as we go about our daily lives.

Humility

Humble yourself as a little child. Matthew 18:4 says, *"Assuredly, I say to you, unless you are converted and become as little children, you will by no means enter the kingdom of heaven. Therefore whoever humbles himself as this little child is the greatest in the kingdom of heaven."*

Christ tells us to humble ourselves and come to Him as a little child. He says that if we don't, we will *"by no means enter the kingdom of heaven."* So once again this is not optional. We must humble ourselves as a little child, or we don't go to heaven. It's as simple as that. In many places throughout the Old and New Testament, God says he hates pride.

For example James 4:6 says, "God resists the proud, But gives grace to the humble." And in Proverbs 16:18, it says, "Pride goes before destruction, and a haughty spirit before a fall."

Furthermore, in Matthew 23:8–12 Jesus says,

> *But you, do not be called "Rabbi"; for One is your Teacher, the Christ, and you are all brethren. Do not call anyone on earth your father; for One is your Father, He who is in heaven. And do not be called teachers; for One is your Teacher, the Christ. But he who is greatest among you shall be your servant. And whoever exalts himself will be humbled, and he who humbles himself will be exalted.*

If your pastor spends a lot of time making himself look good or if he is haughty, then you should probably find a new church. When I was a teenager in Grand Bay, Alabama, our pastor at the First United Methodist Church was called Brother Roberts, not Pastor Roberts, not Reverend Roberts, not Father Roberts, just Brother Roberts. He was a wise man.

Our Words

Jesus tells us the power of our words in Mathew 12:36–37. He says, *"But I say to you that for every idle word men may speak, they will give account of it in the day of judgment. For by your words you will be justified, and by your words you will be condemned."*

Wow, there are a lot of things that I wish I hadn't said! How about you?

The Pharisees were grumbling that Jesus' disciples would eat with unwashed hands, eat the wrong things, etc., and Jesus then replied,

> *Hear and understand: Not what goes into the mouth defiles a man; but what comes out of the mouth, this defiles a man … So Jesus said, "Are you also still without understanding? Do you not yet understand that whatever enters the mouth goes into the stomach and is eliminated? But those things which proceed out of the mouth come from the heart, and they defile a man. For out of the heart proceed evil thoughts, murders, adulteries, fornications, thefts, false witness, blasphemies. These are the things which defile a man, but to eat with unwashed hands does not defile a man."*
> (Matthew 15:10–11, 16–20).

So we need to watch what we think and watch what we say.

The Beatitudes

In Matthew 5, Jesus gives the Sermon on the Mount, and He starts it with the Beatitudes in Matthew 5:3–11.

> *Blessed are the poor in spirit,*
> *For theirs is the kingdom of heaven.*
> *Blessed are those who mourn,*
> *For they shall be comforted.*
> *Blessed are the meek,*
> *For they shall inherit the earth.*
> *Blessed are those who hunger and thirst for righteousness,*
> *For they shall be filled.*

Blessed are the merciful,
For they shall obtain mercy.
Blessed are the pure in heart,
For they shall see God.
Blessed are the peacemakers,
For they shall be called sons of God.
Blessed are those who are persecuted for righteousness' sake,
For theirs is the kingdom of heaven.
Blessed are you when they revile and persecute you,
and say all kinds of evil against you falsely for My sake.

Jesus said all this because it is how He wants us to live, how He expects us to be. Sometimes people forget these things. It is worth spending a little time thinking about each one of these nine statements.

Sin and the Law

Matthew 4:17 says, "From that time Jesus began to preach and to say, *'Repent, for the kingdom of heaven is at hand.'*"

Some people think that because Jesus died for our sins that they can do whatever they want. But Jesus says in Matthew 5:17–18, *"Do not think that I came to destroy the Law or the Prophets. I did not come to destroy but to fulfill. For assuredly, I say to you, till heaven and earth pass away, one jot or one tittle will by no means pass from the law till all is fulfilled."*

So those Ten Commandments are still commandments—that's that.

Sin comes from our hearts. In Matthew 5:21–30, Jesus tells us,

You have heard that it was said to those of old, "You shall not murder, and whoever murders will be in

> *danger of the judgment." But I say to you that whoever*
> *is angry with his brother without a cause shall be in*
> *danger of the judgment ... You have heard that it was*
> *said to those of old, "You shall not commit adultery."*
> *But I say to you that whoever looks at a woman to*
> *lust for her has already committed adultery with her*
> *in his heart.*

If we even think about sinning, then in the eyes of God we have already committed the sin, and we are in danger of judgment. Come on, Jesus. Really? Jeez! Yes, I think He meant what He said. It seems to me that Jesus says what He means, means what He says, and doesn't need a lot of interpretation. In Matthew 5:29-30 Jesus then goes on to say,

> *If your right eye causes you to sin, pluck it out and cast*
> *it from you; for it is more profitable for you that one of*
> *your members perish, than for your whole body to be*
> *cast into hell. And if your right hand causes you to sin,*
> *cut it off and cast it from you; for it is more profitable*
> *for you that one of your members perish, than for your*
> *whole body to be cast into hell.*

So if *anything* in your life causes you to sin, get rid of it, or you will go to hell. Hmmm, I know lots of people these days seem to think God is so loving that He would never cast anyone into hell. Well, that is just wrong. Jesus warns of it here, and as you will see later in this book, He warns us about it over and over again. God does love us; however, He is righteous and hates sin, and that is why He sent Jesus. All we have to do is ask His forgiveness and accept Him as our Lord and Savior and repent of our sins to be saved from hell, but if we don't, if we choose to keep sin in our lives and reject the Lord, then we will burn. Jesus said it over and over, and He wasn't joking around.

What Jesus Said about Cities and Nations

Unrepentant Cities and Nations

Jesus not only expects us as individuals to follow Him, but He also expects cities and nations to follow Him. And He is stern about it.

He condemns wicked cities who reject Him. Matthew 11:20–24 says,

> Then He began to rebuke the cities in which most of His mighty works had been done, because they did not repent: *"Woe to you, Chorazin! Woe to you, Bethsaida! For if the mighty works which were done in you had been done in Tyre and Sidon, they would have repented long ago in sackcloth and ashes. But I say to you, it will be more tolerable for Tyre and Sidon in the day of judgment than for you. And you, Capernaum, who are exalted to heaven, will be brought down to Hades; for if the mighty works which were done in you had been done in Sodom, it would have remained until this day. But I say to you that it shall be more tolerable for the land of Sodom in the day of judgment than for you."*

There are a lot of wicked cities and nations in the world right now, cities and nations that God has historically blessed but that have now forgotten about Him, forgotten about the source of all their wealth, success, and power. To a large extent, Europe and the United States have forgotten that God is the source of all their blessings. That can't go well in the long run. Jesus said so. As Cotton Mather said, "Religion begat prosperity, and the daughter devoured the mother."

There is a warning to nations who reject Christ in Matthew 21:42–44.

> Jesus said to them, *"Have you never read in the Scriptures: 'The stone which the builders rejected has become the chief cornerstone. This was the LORD's doing, and it is marvelous in our eyes'? Therefore I say to you, the kingdom of God will be taken from you and given to a nation bearing the fruits of it. And whoever falls on this stone will be broken; but on whomever it falls, it will grind him to powder."*

Jesus is that cornerstone, and sadly He is being rejected by our nation. That can't work out well for us. If we as a nation continue to reject Him and His Word for the sake of political correctness, we will be "ground to powder." He also says that the kingdom of God will be taken from us and given to another nation *"bearing the fruits of it."* So what does Jesus thinks about our country right now? Our country is now thumbing its nose at the Lord, with President Obama saying that the United States is no longer a Christian nation at a press conference in Turkey in 2009.

Let's see what Frederick Douglas said about politics:

> I have one great Political idea ... Righteousness exalteth a nation; sin is a reproach to any people."
> This constitutes my politics—the negative and positive of my politics, and the whole of my politics ... I feel it my duty to do all in my power to infuse this idea into the public mind.[13]

I have much more to say about this subject, perhaps enough for another book.

Warnings!

Hypocritical Church People

Several times in the book of Matthew, Jesus strongly criticizes hypocritical religious people. I think these verses sum it up both then and now. Jesus quotes Isaiah, *"These people draw near to Me with their mouth, and honor Me with their lips, but their heart is far from Me. And in vain they worship Me, teaching as doctrines the commandments of men"* (Matthew 15:7–9).

This really does describe a lot of churches, and this brings me to my usual discourse about churches and church people. I truly believe that it is important to go to church, to hear the Word of God preached, to learn together, and to fellowship with other believers in Christ in order to support, love, and strengthen one another. I also believe that it is very difficult to find a good church in which to do that. It is important to find a church that really preaches the Word of God as doctrine, not "the commandments of men." Moreover, churches are made up of people, and people are imperfect. Church people, perhaps more than others, tend to be self-righteous, to judge people, and to not be forgiving. Isn't that odd since Jesus commands us not to judge others and to forgive them? But my advice is to go anyway. Find a good Bible-believing church and go in spite of the faults of the church people. Church is important. Worshipping God at home in private is important, but church is just as important. I have heard many people say that they don't like church and that they can worship God in their own ways. It can be done, but it is very difficult. People say that, and after a period of time they drift away from God. It happens every time. The church is the body of Christ. Just go.

Jesus harshly criticizes the religious hypocrites in the Scriptures below.

Matthew 15:12–13 says,

> Then His disciples came and said to Him, "Do You know that the Pharisees were offended when they heard this saying?" But He answered and said, *Every plant which My heavenly Father has not planted will be uprooted. Let them alone. They are blind leaders of the blind. And if the blind leads the blind, both will fall into a ditch."*

And in Matthew 7:21–23 Jesus says,

> *Not everyone who says to Me, "Lord, Lord," shall enter the kingdom of heaven, but he who does the will of My Father in heaven. Many will say to Me in that day, "Lord, Lord, have we not prophesied in Your name, cast out demons in Your name, and done many wonders in Your name?" And then I will declare to them, "I never knew you; depart from Me, you who practice lawlessness!"*

This is addressed to the religious people, those good churchgoing people who don't really have a relationship with Christ. They just go to church, and they are good people; however, they don't really know the Lord. So it's important to be sure you really know Him. It's kind of scary.

In Matthew 21:31–32 Jesus says,

> *Assuredly, I say to you that tax collectors and harlots enter the kingdom of God before you. For John came to you in the way of righteousness, and you did not believe him; but tax collectors and harlots believed him; and when you saw it, you did not afterward relent and believe him.*

So if you think that you are good enough and that you don't need Jesus, then the wicked sinners may get into heaven, but you won't. Remember, the worst sin of all is rejecting God.

The entirety of Matthew 23 is about the hypocrisy of church leaders. I will spare you the details. You can read it for yourself. It is very condemning. Jesus doesn't like religious hypocrites any more than we do. Enough said.

The Straight and Narrow Path

In Mathew 7:13–14 Jesus says, *"Enter by the narrow gate; for wide is the gate and broad is the way that leads to destruction, and there are many who go in by it. Because narrow is the gate and difficult is the way which leads to life, and there are few who find it."*

Jesus is the narrow gate that leads to life. Any other way is the broad way that leads to destruction. People just hate to hear that, but that is what Jesus is saying. In the words of Hank Williams Sr.,

> I was a fool to wander and stray
> Straight is the gate and narrow the way
> Now I have traded the wrong for the right
> Praise the Lord I saw the light.

Beware of false prophets. In Matthew 7:15 Jesus says, *"Beware of false prophets, who come to you in sheep's clothing, but inwardly they are ravenous wolves."*

Ever wonder where that old saying "A wolf in sheep's clothing" came from? It came from Jesus. There are all kinds of spiritual leaders in the world today, professing all kinds of theologies, and of course, they all come across as good, speaking of goodness and kindness toward your fellow man, inner peace and harmony, tapping into the energy of the universe, etc. Frankly I think anybody can say all that stuff. Sure it sounds good, but Jesus warns us that they are "ravenous wolves." Why? Because they are not preaching the gospel of Jesus Christ. They are misleading you, taking you down the wrong road, leading you to destruction. Yes, this includes all the other major religions—Buddhism, Hinduism, Islam, etc. They are all false prophets, all wolves in sheep's clothing, ravenous wolves sent to destroy you. Yes, I'm saying they are wrong and that they lead you through the *"wide gate"* and down the *"broad path"* that leads to the destruction of your soul by convincing you to put your faith in someone or something other than Jesus Christ, someone other than the one true God, Jehovah. Jesus says that *"no one comes to the Father except through Me."* (John 14:6) Just look at what He said in the previous verses, *"Enter by the narrow gate."* Jesus Christ is that gate.

It is a sad fact that Jesus comes to us and tells us the truth, and yet people don't like what they hear and don't want to believe. It's like Jesus said in Matthew 13:57, *"A prophet is not without honor except in his own country and in his own house."* Instead, they literally seek out false prophets who tell them what they want to hear. The apostle Paul predicted this in 2 Timothy 4:3, which says "For the time will come when they will not endure sound doctrine, but according to their own desires, because they have itching ears, they will heap up for themselves teachers, and they will turn their ears away from the truth, and be turned aside to fables." Ravi Zacharis gives a very good description of this in his book, *Why Jesus?* He states, "Now we have lost Him because we prefer to live a lie rather than the truth; we prefer to believe that we are gods ourselves when, in truth, we are the glory of creation gone wrong. We have set up a context of rebellion against Him and are therefore no longer on the side of truth. Jesus makes a sweeping statement that our true intentions regarding truth or falsehood are revealed in what we do with Him."[14]

Jesus Christ is right there in front of us, speaking the truth. He said. *"I am the Truth,"* and yet people run to psychics and mediums and to the Dalai Lama, to cults like Scientology, and Universalism, etc. We run to the ravenous wolves. People are rebellious, saying, "No, Christ can't be right. I have to rebel and find my own way." It is stupidity. The truth is right in front of us. We only need to accept Him.

There is one God. His name is Jehovah. He sent His Son, Jesus Christ, to die for our sins and to save our souls and to bring us into a true relationship with God. Jesus is the only way to get there. He tells us that over and over. He makes it very clear. Either He's telling the truth, or He's a liar. As for me, I know He's telling the truth. We'll explore this in Chapter 3.

Warning about False Messiahs and False Prophets, the Second Coming, and the End Times

The disciples asked Jesus about His second coming. Here is what He said:

> Now as He sat on the Mount of Olives, the disciples came to Him privately, saying, "Tell us, when will these things be? And what will be the sign of Your coming, and of the end of the age?" And Jesus answered and said to them: *"Take heed that no one deceives you. For many will come in My name, saying, 'I am the Christ,' and will deceive many. And you will hear of wars and rumors of wars. See that you are not troubled; for all these things must come to pass, but the end is not yet. For nation will rise against nation, and kingdom against kingdom. And there will be famines, pestilences, and earthquakes in various places. All these are the beginning of sorrows. Then they will deliver*

you up to tribulation and kill you, and you will be hated by all nations for My name's sake. And then many will be offended, will betray one another, and will hate one another. Then many false prophets will rise up and deceive many. And because lawlessness will abound, the love of many will grow cold. But he who endures to the end shall be saved. And this gospel of the kingdom will be preached in all the world as a witness to all the nations, and then the end will come ... Then if anyone says to you, 'Look, here is the Christ!' or 'There!' do not believe it. For false christs and false prophets will rise and show great signs and wonders to deceive, if possible, even the elect. See, I have told you beforehand ... But of that day and hour no one knows, not even the angels of heaven, but My Father only. But as the days of Noah were, so also will the coming of the Son of Man be. For as in the days before the flood, they were eating and drinking, marrying and giving in marriage, until the day that Noah entered the ark, and did not know until the flood came and took them all away, so also will the coming of the Son of Man be. Then two men will be in the field: one will be taken and the other left. Two women will be grinding at the mill: one will be taken and the other left. Watch therefore, for you do not know what hour your Lord is coming. But know this, that if the master of the house had known what hour the thief would come, he would have watched and not allowed his house to be broken into. Therefore you also be ready, for the Son of Man is coming at an hour you do not expect." (Matthew 24:3–14, 23–25, 36–44)

Beware of false prophets, those spiritual teachers who tell you what you want to hear. Know Christ so that you really know the Truth and are not deceived by others. Jesus is coming back. He said He will *"come on the clouds of heaven with power and great glory,"* but if anyone says that he knows when Jesus is coming back, don't believe him. By definition, that person is a false prophet. Jesus tells us to just be ready. In order to be ready, we need to be saved. We need to be born again and be in the right relationship with God.

Persecution

In Matthew 5:11 Jesus says, *"Blessed are you when they revile and persecute you, and say all kinds of evil against you falsely for My sake."*

In Matthew 10:17–22 Jesus then says,

> *But beware of men, for they will deliver you up to councils and scourge you in their synagogues. You will be brought before governors and kings for My sake, as a testimony to them and to the Gentiles. But when they deliver you up, do not worry about how or what you should speak. For it will be given to you in that hour what you should speak; for it is not you who speak, but the Spirit of your Father who speaks in you. Now brother will deliver up brother to death, and a father his child; and children will rise up against parents and cause them to be put to death. And you will be hated by all for My name's sake. But he who endures to the end will be saved.*

Yes, people will criticize you and hate you for your belief in Christ. Jesus tells us not to worry about what to say in response. He says that it will be given to you by the Holy Spirit. In my personal experience this is very true. When someone challenges my belief and I try to respond on my own, I flounder, but if I let the Holy Spirit speak through me, it works. I have found that it is no use to share my faith with someone whom I think needs to hear it. That does not work; however, often God will send me to someone or send someone to me, and the person will approach me. Then if I let the Holy Spirit speak through me, it works. There is a great book about this titled *You Were Born for This* by Bruce Wilkinson.[15]

Resist the Devil

Matthew 16:23 says, "But He turned and said to Peter, *'Get behind Me, Satan! You are an offense to Me, for you are not mindful of the things of God, but the things of men.'*"

Peter had good intentions. He was trying to help. He wanted to protect Jesus from crucifixion. That sounds admirable. But Jesus knew that it was God's plan that He die on the cross. So there is an important lesson here. When you know what you should do, when you know what God wants you to do, sometimes good people who love and care about you and who have good intentions will try to stop you. You must override them.

Hell

Nobody wants to talk about this one, but we must. Jesus warns us about hell more than seventy times in the New Testament. You probably noticed some of those warnings previously in this book. Let's look again.

In Matthew 10:28 Jesus says,

> *And do not fear those who kill the body but cannot kill the soul. But rather fear Him who is able to destroy both soul and body in hell.*

In Matthew 25:41–43 He then says,

> *Then He will also say to those on the left hand, "Depart from Me, you cursed, into the everlasting fire prepared for the devil and his angels: for I was hungry and you gave Me no food; I was thirsty and you gave Me no drink; I was a stranger and you did not take Me in, naked and you did not clothe Me, sick and in prison and you did not visit Me."*

In Matthew 25:46 He goes on to say,

> *And these will go away into everlasting punishment, but the righteous into eternal life.*

In Matthew 18:8–9 Jesus states,

> *If your hand or foot causes you to sin, cut it off and cast it from you. It is better for you to enter into life lame or maimed, rather than having two hands or two feet, to be cast into the everlasting fire. And if your eye causes you to sin, pluck it out and cast it from you. It is better for you to enter into life with one eye, rather than having two eyes, to be cast into hell fire.*

In Matthew 13:41–42 He says,

> *"The Son of Man will send out His angels, and they will gather out of His kingdom all things that offend, and those who practice lawlessness, and will cast them into the furnace of fire. There will be wailing and gnashing of teeth."*

In addition to these very direct warnings about hell, Jesus also uses more indirect terms, such as the *judgment* or *destruction*, or He says, *"Deliver you to the torturers."*

Jesus repeatedly tells us to follow Him, do what He says, or burn in hell. These are His words, not mine, not some preacher's statements either. I don't like hearing that, but these are the words of Jesus Christ, the Son of God, the Messiah, the Savior. I know many people who just don't believe this. They say things like, "God loves everyone. He wouldn't send anyone to hell." That is just crazy. It is denial. I've read that 90 percent of Americans believe in heaven and only 30 percent believe in hell. (A. Stanley, 2003)

Do you think Jesus is a liar? Do you think He didn't really mean it when he gave us all these warnings? If you don't believe what He taught, then you are saying He is a liar. I'll ask you again. Is He a liar? It's hard to say that, isn't it? You kind of choke on those words, don't you? I've seen it before. When people tell me that they think Jesus was a great teacher, they will simultaneously say they don't believe the things He taught, don't believe they need to be saved, and don't believe what He said about hell, or they say that they don't believe that He is the only way to God (John 14:6). So then I'll ask, "Do you think He is a liar?" They squirm, and they get defensive.

Read what C. S. Lewis said about this in his book *Mere Christianity*:

> I am trying here to prevent anyone saying the really foolish thing that people often say about Him: I'm ready to accept Jesus as a great moral teacher, but I don't accept his claim to be God. That is the one thing we must not say. A man who was merely a man and said the sort of things Jesus said would not be a great moral teacher. He would either be a lunatic—on the level with the man who says he is

a poached egg—or else he would be the Devil of
Hell. You must make your choice. Either this man
was, and is, the Son of God, or else a madman or
something worse. You can shut him up for a fool,
you can spit at him and kill him as a demon or
you can fall at his feet and call him Lord and God,
but let us not come with any patronizing nonsense
about his being a great human teacher. He has not
left that open to us. He did not intend to.

In his book *Radical: Taking Back Your Faith from the American
Dream*, David Platt states, "He is the sovereign Lord. He doesn't
give options for people to consider; He gives commands for people
to obey."

So with all of these warnings about hell, we should talk about how
to avoid it. That is the major theme of the next chapter.

CHAPTER 3

Read John to Save Your Soul

Jesus answered and said to him, *"Most assuredly, I say to you,
unless one is born again, he cannot see the kingdom of God."*
—JOHN 3:3

WHO IS JESUS AND WHY DID HE COME?

At the beginning of chapter 2 I mentioned that the dominant theme
of the gospel of John is the description of who Jesus is and why He
came. Let's take a look at John's introduction to Jesus.

John 1:1–5 says,

> In the beginning was the Word, and the Word was
> with God, and the Word was God. He was in the
> beginning with God. All things were made through
> Him, and without Him nothing was made that was
> made. In Him was life, and the life was the light of
> men. And the light shines in the darkness, and the
> darkness did not comprehend it.

And John 1:10-13 says,

> He was in the world, and the world was made
> through Him, and the world did not know Him.
> He came to His own, and His own did not receive
> Him. But as many as received Him, to them He
> gave the right to become children of God, to those
> who believe in His name: who were born, not of
> blood, nor of the will of the flesh, nor of the will of
> man, but of God.

So Jesus is the Word. Jesus was with God. Jesus is God. Through Him all things were made. He is the light in the darkness, and He gave us the right to become children of God *if* we receive Him and *if* we believe in Him. You see, in order to become children of God, we must receive *and* believe.

Okay, so that's what John said about Jesus. Throughout this chapter you will see what Jesus said about Himself. He said that He is the Light of the World, that He is Living Water, that He gives everlasting life, that He is the Bread of Life, that He is the Good Shepherd, that He is the True Vine, that He is the Son of God. He said that He and the Father are One and that He came down from heaven. He said that He was sent to do the will of the Father. He said that He is the Messiah, the Christ, and that He came to save us.

At the end of the previous chapter I pointed out several of the warnings that Jesus gave us, and I then said we would discuss how to avoid hell, the torturers, the fiery furnace, the eternal fire, which Jesus had warned us about so many times. So let's see what Jesus said about that.

WHAT JESUS SAID ABOUT SALVATION

Why We Need to Be Saved

Jesus said He came to save us because we are already condemned! Everyone knows John 3:16–17, which says,

> *For God so loved the world that He gave His only begotten Son, that whoever believes in Him should not perish but have everlasting life. For God did not send His Son into the world to condemn the world, but that the world through Him might be saved.*

God loves us. He gave His only Son, and *if* we believe in Him, *if* we receive Him, *if* we have faith in Him, we will not perish, but instead we will live forever. Wonderful, isn't it? It is beautiful. It is comforting. It is the very foundation of the Christian faith. It makes you feel all warm and fuzzy inside. But everyone seems to stop reading right there, or perhaps they forget the rest of it. Read John 3:18–19, which says,

> *He who believes in Him is not condemned; but he who does not believe is condemned already, because he has not believed in the name of the only begotten Son of God. And this is the condemnation, that the light has come into the world, and men loved darkness rather than light, because their deeds were evil.*

So Jesus said if we do not believe in Him, the Son of God, that we are condemned already. That is why we need to be saved. Later in His closing statement in chapter 3, Jesus said,

> *"He who believes in the Son has everlasting life; and he who does not believe the Son shall not see life, but the wrath of God abides on him"* (John 3:36).

Once again He's being very stern here. Believe in Christ, and you get everlasting life. Don't believe, and the wrath of God will abide on you. You really don't want the wrath of God to abide on you. That would hurt!

As I mentioned in the previous chapter, I have friends who say, "I don't feel I need to be saved. I am a good person." Okay, but Jesus makes it clear, "He who does not believe in Him is condemned already." It has nothing to do with being a good person by human standards. What is strange to me is that so many people really hate that statement. They would rather try to be good, at least relative to bad people, than to believe in Christ as their Savior. It is stupid. You cannot possibly be good enough to get to heaven. It cannot happen. Proverbs 14:12 says, "There is a way that seems right to a man, but it's end is the way of death." If you don't believe that you need to be saved, read Andy Stanley's book *How Good Is Good Enough?*. He explains this much better than I do. There is also a fantastic book by Ray Comfort titled *God Has a Wonderful Plan for Your Life: The Myth of the Modern Message*. Ray uses the Ten Commandments to show us all that we need to repent and what we need for salvation.

C.S. Lewis discusses this in *Mere Christianity*, explaining that being good and being nice is not good enough, and in fact, that makes it more difficult to be saved. If you realize that you are a sinner, then you have a chance, but if you think you are good, you're in big trouble. He states,

> If you mistake for your own merits what are really
> God's gifts to you through nature, and if you are
> contented with simply being nice, you are still a
> rebel; and all those gifts will only make your fall
> more terrible, your corruption more complicated,
> your bad example more disastrous. The devil was an
> archangel once; his natural gifts were as far above

yours as yours are above a chimpanzee … A world of nice people, content in their own niceness, looking no further, turned away from God, would be just as desperately in need of salvation as a miserable world—and might be more difficult to save. For mere improvement is not redemption, though redemption always improves.

This is serious stuff, so I will once again ask, "Do you think Jesus is lying?" By the way, fifty times in the book of John Jesus tells us that He is telling the truth. He says that you must be born again or you won't see the kingdom of heaven. He said that if you don't believe Him, you will experience the wrath of God. Do you think He is lying, or is He telling the truth? I happen to know He is telling the truth.

How are we Saved?

Jesus said you must be born again. John 3:1–6 says,

There was a man of the Pharisees named Nicodemus, a ruler of the Jews. This man came to Jesus by night and said to Him, "Rabbi, we know that You are a teacher come from God; for no one can do these signs that You do unless God is with him." Jesus answered and said to him, *"Most assuredly, I say to you, unless one is born again, he cannot see the kingdom of God."* Nicodemus said to Him, "How can a man be born when he is old? Can he enter a second time into his mother's womb and be born?" Jesus answered, *"Most assuredly, I say to you, unless one is born of water and the Spirit, he cannot enter the kingdom of God. That which is born of the flesh is flesh, and that which is born of the Spirit is spirit."*

So that settles it. Jesus told Nicodemus that *"unless one is born again he cannot see the kingdom of God."* And He later tells us what that means is to be *"born of the Spirit,"* meaning the Holy Spirit. So He is saying this is *mandatory.* It is not optional. If you want to have everlasting life and not burn in the fiery furnace, then you must be born again.

A few of my friends have asked me, "What does it mean to be born again?" They think born-again Christians are just right-wing radical wackos who are judgmental and intolerant of others. They think that these people go crazy in church, yelling, jumping up and down, getting bopped on the head, and falling on the floor. It is easy to see why they think that, but that is not it at all. I think the best way to explain this is just to tell you how it happened for me.

I was fifteen years old, and my mother insisted that I go to church camp for one week that summer. I thought that was really lame. I did not want to go. I wanted to stay home, race horses, hang out with my friends, and chase girls. (Hmmm, maybe I was lame.) Once I got to church camp, I actually started listening to the preachers, and wow, I felt convicted by the Holy Spirit, not by my conscience, not by the words of the preacher, but actually by the Spirit of God. Seriously, I was not convicted by man but by God. There is a huge difference. I really knew that I was a sinner. I knew that I had not kept the Ten Commandments and that I needed forgiveness. On my last night there I still had not accepted Christ as my Savior, and I was troubled. I left the dorm at about one in the morning, went down to the lake, sat on a bench, and prayed. I prayed for what seemed like hours, totally humbling myself before the Lord Jesus Christ, begging for His forgiveness. (Remember, He said *"If you do not humble yourself as a little child you will by no means enter the kingdom of heaven."*) I was literally begging. It seemed hopeless, and then suddenly it happened. He came to me, forgave me, washed away all my sins, and I was filled with the Holy Spirit. I was born again, saved, washed in the blood! It is real! I know it is hard to understand. I did not understand it until it happened to me, but this is not just some emotion. It really happens. I cannot stress this enough. Literally when Jesus forgives you, you are born again, born of the Spirit, and filled with the Holy Spirit. At that moment you know that you have a soul, and something very real happens to your spirit. It is almost physical. This is not some whacky thing that crazy religious people do (although there are a lot of those wackos). This is salvation. This is redemption. This is getting right with God.

At that same moment I was overwhelmed by the love of God for me. That aspect of salvation is very emotional and very real. The Holy Spirit gave me a new heart, and I knew at that moment that I was truly a blessed child of God.

If you ask most Protestant preachers what it means to be born again, they will tell you it is three or four steps as follows:

1. Ask Jesus to forgive you of your sins.

2. Repent of your sins.

3. Accept Christ as your Lord and Savior (Really ask Him to be the Lord of your life.)

4. Then you are born again, filled with the Holy Spirit, and born of the Spirit. You are Saved!

Catholics have a different approach to this. They agree that you must be born again. After all, Christ said it. They just do it differently. Catholics believe that you are saved by baptism. It is at the sacrament of confirmation that they are filled with the Holy Spirit and born of the Spirit. That's when they are confirmed.

I don't care about these theological differences between Catholics and Protestants. What I am confident of is that when it happens to you, you will know it. If you did not knowingly receive the Holy Spirit, you are not born again. I absolutely believe that there are plenty of false converts in both Catholic and Protestant churches—people who claim to be Christians and even believe that they are Christians but are not because they have not been born again, have not given their lives to Christ and received Him as their Savior, and have not made Him the Lord of their lives. Read Matthew 7:21–23 again,

> *Not everyone who says to Me, "Lord, Lord," shall enter the kingdom of heaven, but he who does the will of My Father in heaven. Many will say to Me in that day, "Lord, Lord, have we not prophesied in Your name, cast out demons in Your name, and done many wonders in Your name?" And then I will declare to them, "I never knew you; depart from Me, you who practice lawlessness!"*

Let me clarify the word *lawlessness*. This does not refer to a criminal here on earth who is breaking the laws of man. This means breaking God's laws, e.g., breaking the first commandment by not putting God first in your life. Have you ever done that? Martin Luther said that if we keep the first commandment, we won't break the rest of them.[16] Have you ever taken the Lord's name in vain or not kept the Sabbath holy? Have you ever had adulterous thoughts or hated someone or coveted someone else's stuff or been disrespectful to your parents or lied or cheated? This is what God means by lawlessness. If you have ever done any of that, then you are a sinner. You are condemned, and you need salvation. We all need salvation.

So the point is that it is important to repent and to be born again so that you will be in right relationship with God through Christ.

Going to church and being a good person doesn't cut it, not even close. If that were enough, Jesus would not have had to die for our sins, but He did. We need only to accept Him.

What happens when you are Born Again?

Once you accept Christ and are born again, then you will be able to enter the kingdom of God (John 3:5), and you will not have the wrath of God abide on you (John3:36). That's good! In addition to going to heaven and not burning in hell, you get several really cool perks.

You receive the Holy Spirit

John 14:23–24 says,

> Jesus answered and said to him, *"If anyone loves Me, he will keep My word; and My Father will love him, and We will come to him and make Our home with him. He who does not love Me does not keep My words; and the word which you hear is not Mine but the Father's who sent Me."*

This is key. This is what Christianity is all about—that God the Father and God the Son literally live in you in the form of the Holy Spirit. To the nonbeliever, this sounds absolutely crazy. I don't think you can understand this until it happens to you. Once it does, you know it is the truth.

Lewis describes it this way:

> Put right out of your head the idea that these are only fancy ways of saying Christians are to read

what Christ said and try to carry it out—as a man might read Plato or Marx and try to carry it out. They mean something much more than that. They mean that a real Person, Jesus Christ, here and now, in that very room, where you are saying your prayers, is doing things to you. It is not a question of a good man who died 2000 years ago. It is a living man, still as much a man as you, and still as much God as when he created the world, really coming and interfering with your very self; killing the old natural self in you, and replacing it with the kind of self he has. At first, only for moments. Then for longer periods. Finally, if all goes well, turning you permanently into a different sort of thing; into a new little Christ, a being which shares in His power, joy, knowledge, and eternity.

Earlier I said that when you are born again and saved, you become filled with the Holy Spirit. Here's what Jesus said about the Holy Spirit in John 14:15-18,

> *If you love Me, keep My commandments. And I will pray the Father, and He will give you another Helper, that He may abide with you forever—the Spirit of truth, whom the world cannot receive, because it neither sees Him nor knows Him; but you know Him, for He dwells with you and will be in you. I will not leave you orphans; I will come to you.*

In John 14:26 Jesus then says,

> *But the Helper, the Holy Spirit, whom the Father will send in My name, He will teach you all things, and bring to your remembrance all things that I said to you.*

In John 15:26–27 He states,

> *But when the Helper comes, whom I shall send to you from the Father, the Spirit of truth who proceeds from the Father, He will testify of Me. And you also will bear witness, because you have been with Me from the beginning.*

So once Jesus died, He sent the Holy Spirit to be with us, and abide in us forever. He said the Holy Spirit will teach us all things and will remind us of all the things Jesus said. As He promised, He did not leave us orphans. Just like the old hymn says, "He lives, He lives, Christ Jesus lives today. He walks with me, and talks with me, along life's narrow way." To the born-again believer, the Holy Spirit is his or her guide. He lives in us, helps us to make decisions according to God's will, and guides our path *if* we listen to Him. Many people and many Christians don't listen. For about twenty years or so I wasn't listening, and that was stupid.

In *How to Listen to God*, Charles Stanley writes, "There is no way for us to hear from God apart from the ministry of the Holy Spirit." And later he says,

> To receive God's direction we must have a right relationship with Him. That relationship means that we must be filled with the Holy Spirit, and we must learn to walk in His Spirit, not grieving the Holy Spirit of God (see Eph. 4:30) If we grieve the Holy Spirit of God, by saying yes to sin and quench the Spirit by saying no to God, how can the Holy Spirit who is both receiver and communicator to our spirits declare God's revelation? One of the primary reasons people do not hear from God is because they are not living in the Spirit. Their lifestyle is one of quiet rebellion against God.

If you keep rebelling against God by not accepting Christ and not making Him the Lord of your life, then you won't hear from God. You must submit your will to Him. Then it works!

The Holy Spirit convicts the world of sin. In John 16:7–11 Jesus says,

> *Nevertheless I tell you the truth. It is to your advantage that I go away; for if I do not go away, the Helper will not come to you; but if I depart, I will send Him to you. And when He has come, He will convict the world of sin, and of righteousness, and of judgment: of sin, because they do not believe in Me; of righteousness, because I go to My Father and you see Me no more; of judgment, because the ruler of this world is judged.*

Did you catch that? Jesus said that the Holy Spirit *"will convict the world of sin, and righteousness, and of judgment; of sin because they do not believe in Me."* He tells us that the only way to be saved from sin is to believe in Jesus Christ and to accept Him as our Savior.

The Holy Spirit is also the spirit of truth. In John 16:13–15 Jesus says,

> *However, when He, the Spirit of truth, has come, He will guide you into all truth; for He will not speak on His own authority, but whatever He hears He will speak; and He will tell you things to come. He will glorify Me, for He will take of what is Mine and declare it to you. All things that the Father has are Mine. Therefore I said that He will take of Mine and declare it to you.*

Yes, the Holy Spirit is our helper. He lives in us. He leads us and guides us in truth if we accept Christ and if we listen to Him. He reminds us of all things Jesus said. He glorifies Christ, and He will take what is Christ's and declare it to us. He is giving to us the right to become children of God and to have all things that the Son of God has. Cool!

Charles Stanley's book *How to Listen to God* gives a very good description of the Holy Spirit and the many ways that God speaks to us through the Holy Spirit. He also points out that this only happens after you are born again, not before. Yes, I know many people don't like to hear that, but it is true.

You get Everlasting Life

Jesus said that if we believe in Him, He will give us everlasting life. That's a pretty nice bonus! We just read in John 3:15–16 and John 3:36 that Jesus offers us everlasting life if we believe in Him. This message is repeated by Jesus in the Scriptures below.

John 4:13-14 says,

> Jesus answered and said to her, '*Whoever drinks of this water will thirst again, but whoever drinks of the water that I shall give him will never thirst. But the water that I shall give him will become in him a fountain of water springing up into everlasting life.*'

In John 6:40 Jesus says,

> *And this is the will of Him who sent Me, that everyone who sees the Son and believes in Him may have everlasting life; and I will raise him up at the last day.*

In John 6:47–48 Jesus then says,

> *Most assuredly, I say to you, he who believes in Me has everlasting life. I am the bread of life.*

In John 6:51 He states,

> *I am the living bread which came down from heaven.*
> *If anyone eats of this bread, he will live forever.*

In John 8:51 He tells us,

> *Most assuredly, I say to you, if anyone keeps My word*
> *he shall never see death.*

And John 11:25–27 says,

> Jesus said to her, *"I am the resurrection and the life.*
> *He who believes in Me, though he may die, he shall*
> *live. And whoever lives and believes in Me shall never*
> *die. Do you believe this?"* She said to Him, "Yes,
> Lord, I believe that You are the Christ, the Son of
> God, who is to come into the world."

Jesus says that He will give you everlasting life, that you will not die,
and that He will lift you up on the last day if you believe in Him.
That's right. Jesus is the one who will lift you up to heaven on the
last day, not somebody else.

We Get Nourishment for Our Souls

Jesus also says that he is the Bread of Life and that He is the Living
Water. In other words, He is nourishment for our souls.

John 4:10–14 says,

> Jesus answered and said to her, *"If you knew the*
> *gift of God, and who it is who says to you, 'Give Me*
> *a drink,' you would have asked Him, and He would*

> *have given you living water ... Whoever drinks of*
> *this water will thirst again, but whoever drinks of*
> *the water that I shall give him will never thirst. But*
> *the water that I shall give him will become in him a*
> *fountain of water springing up into everlasting life."*

If you thirst for life, come to Christ as it says in John 7:37–38. "On the last day, that great day of the feast, Jesus stood and cried out, saying, *'If anyone thirsts, let him come to Me and drink. He who believes in Me, as the Scripture has said, out of his heart will flow rivers of living water.'"*

Furthermore, John 6:32–40 says,

> Then Jesus said to them, *"Most assuredly, I say to*
> *you, Moses did not give you the bread from heaven,*
> *but My Father gives you the true bread from heaven.*
> *For the bread of God is He who comes down from*
> *heaven and gives life to the world."* Then they said to
> Him, "Lord, give us this bread always." And Jesus
> said to them, *"I am the bread of life. He who comes*
> *to Me shall never hunger, and he who believes in Me*
> *shall never thirst. But I said to you that you have seen*
> *Me and yet do not believe. All that the Father gives*
> *Me will come to Me, and the one who comes to Me I*
> *will by no means cast out. For I have come down from*
> *heaven, not to do My own will, but the will of Him*
> *who sent Me. This is the will of the Father who sent*
> *Me, that of all He has given Me I should lose nothing,*
> *but should raise it up at the last day. And this is the*
> *will of Him who sent Me, that everyone who sees the*
> *Son and believes in Him may have everlasting life; and*
> *I will raise him up at the last day."*

This is very clear. We need spiritual nourishment to feed our souls, and we get that nourishment from Christ. If you don't go to Jesus for that nourishment, your soul will wither and die. But if we eat and drink of Christ, we get everlasting life. He says that if we come to Him, He won't cast us out. He says that God wants us to do this, that it is not God's will that anyone should be lost. He wants to save everyone. And yet He also says that some of us refuse to believe (more on that later).

Communion

John 6:43–58 says,

> Jesus therefore answered and said to them, *"Do not murmur among yourselves. No one can come to Me unless the Father who sent Me draws him; and I will raise him up at the last day. It is written in the prophets, 'And they shall all be taught by God.' Therefore everyone who has heard and learned from the Father comes to Me. Not that anyone has seen the Father, except He who is from God; He has seen the Father. Most assuredly, I say to you, he who believes in Me has everlasting life. I am the bread of life. Your fathers ate the manna in the wilderness, and are dead. This is the bread which comes down from heaven, that one may eat of it and not die. I am the living bread which came down from heaven. If anyone eats of this bread, he will live forever; and the bread that I shall give is My flesh, which I shall give for the life of the world."* The Jews therefore quarreled among themselves, saying, "How can this Man give us His flesh to eat?" Then Jesus said to them, *"Most assuredly, I say to you, unless you eat the flesh of the*

Son of Man and drink His blood, you have no life in you. Whoever eats My flesh and drinks My blood has eternal life, and I will raise him up at the last day. For My flesh is food indeed, and My blood is drink indeed. He who eats My flesh and drinks My blood abides in Me, and I in him. As the living Father sent Me, and I live because of the Father, so he who feeds on Me will live because of Me. This is the bread which came down from heaven—not as your fathers ate the manna, and are dead. He who eats this bread will live forever."

This is why we celebrate Communion (Eucharist). Some believe this is symbolic. Others believe this is literal, that the bread and the wine miraculously become the body and the blood of Christ. It is no matter to me. What matters is that you believe and that you receive this spiritual food from Christ. Notice that He says if you do this, you *"abide in Him, and He abides in you,"* and He says that you will live because of Him. In verse 53, He says that if you don't take Communion, *"you have no life in you."* That is why the Catholics are so serious about it, and I am not sure why some Protestants aren't. When you do receive Christ, you realize that He truly is the Bread of Life, and fountains of Living Water do spring forth from you.

For me Communion is a deeply spiritual act. I remember my first Communion at the First United Methodist Church in Mt. Pulaski, Illinois. It was the first time I remember feeling very close to God. As a child, there are things that you just know but do not understand. This is one of them. Atheists think that kids are brainwashed when they are taught Christianity. That is hogwash. As a child, you simply know it is truth. You do not understand it, but you know God is there. You know God is with you. Communion has been important to me ever since.

There is one more thing I need to point out from these passages. Take another look at John 6:45, which says, *"It is written in the prophets, 'And they shall all be taught by God. Therefore everyone who has heard and learned from the Father comes to Me.'"* If you have learned from the Father, you will come to Christ. If you haven't learned from the Father, you don't come. So how do you learn from the Father? You learn from the Father by reading the Word, praying, and listening to the Word of God preached. Go back and reread chapter 2 on Matthew and listening to God.

You Get Light!

Jesus is the light of the world. In John 9:5 Jesus says, *"As long as I am in the world, I am the light of the world."*

John 12:44–50 then says,

> Then Jesus cried out and said, *"He who believes in Me, believes not in Me but in Him who sent Me. And he who sees Me sees Him who sent Me. I have come as a light into the world, that whoever believes in Me should not abide in darkness. And if anyone hears My words and does not believe, I do not judge him; for I did not come to judge the world but to save the world. He who rejects Me, and does not receive My words, has that which judges him—the word that I have spoken will judge him in the last day. For I have not spoken on My own authority; but the Father who sent Me gave Me a command, what I should say and what I should speak. And I know that His command is everlasting life. Therefore, whatever I speak, just as the Father has told Me, so I speak."*

John 8:12 also states, "Then Jesus spoke to them again, saying, *"I am the light of the world. He who follows Me shall not walk in darkness, but have the light of life."*

Jesus will be a light to our path if we believe in Him, listen to Him, and obey Him. If we don't believe or if we refuse to listen, then we're in the dark. And remember, in Psalm 119:105, King David said, "Your word is a lamp to my feet, and a light to my path." The apostle John said that Jesus is the Word in the flesh. Many people think they can see just fine without Jesus, but to those who think that they do not need His light, He says, *"If you were blind, you would have no sin, but now you say 'we see', therefore your sin remains."*(John 9:41)

You Get Love and Joy

In John 15:9–12 Jesus says,

> *As the Father loved Me, I also have loved you; abide in My love. If you keep My commandments, you will abide in My love, just as I have kept My Father's commandments and abide in His love. These things I have spoken to you, that My joy may remain in you, and that your joy may be full. This is My commandment, that you love one another as I have loved you.*

In John 16:27–28 Jesus says,

> *For the Father Himself loves you, because you have loved Me, and have believed that I came forth from God. I came forth from the Father and have come into the world. Again, I leave the world and go to the Father.*

We should love one another. In John 13:34–35 Jesus says,

> *A new commandment I give to you, that you love one another; as I have loved you, that you also love one another. By this all will know that you are My disciples, if you have love for one another.*

So why does God love you? Jesus said that God loves you because you love Jesus. There you have it. And what else do we need to do? We must abide in His love and keep His commandments. As you recall, Jesus' commandments are to love the Lord, your God, with all your heart and soul and mind and to love your neighbor as yourself. To get God's love, we must love Jesus. We must abide in His love, and we must keep His commandments. By doing that, people will know that we are His disciples. That is what He says. You can't get it any other way, not by doing yoga or tuning in to the energy of the universe. It can't happen.

Now I know that people will say that they can have love and joy without Jesus. Well, to a certain extent, yes, you can get those things here on earth, and they are good; however, I can tell you from personal experience that it is by no means the same as God's love, and to get God's love, we must do these things that Jesus told us above.

You Get Truth and Freedom

John 8:31–36 says,

> Then Jesus said to those Jews who believed Him, *"If you abide in My word, you are My disciples indeed. And you shall know the truth, and the truth shall make you free."* They answered Him, "We are Abraham's descendants, and have never been in bondage to

anyone. How can You say, 'You will be made free'?" Jesus answered them, *"Most assuredly, I say to you, whoever commits sin is a slave of sin. And a slave does not abide in the house forever, but a son abides forever. Therefore if the Son makes you free, you shall be free indeed."*

This is pretty clear. Jesus will forgive our sins if we repent and ask Him. If we do, we abide in the house of the Lord as children of God, and if we don't, then we are slaves to sin. Now please remember, the term sin does not mean breaking the laws of man or being a bad person. It means breaking God's laws, the greatest of which is the first commandment. Once again the greatest sin is not putting God first in our lives. The other sins follow from that.

You become a Child of God

Notice that in John 8:35, He says a son abides in the house forever. Yes, He will make us sons of God. It is not automatic for every human. Jesus says that privilege is given to those who abide in His Word. Jesus said that He will grant us all things that are His. John 16:15 says, *"All things that the Father has are Mine. Therefore I said that He (the Holy Spirit) will take of Mine and declare it to you."*

As a child of God, you get to live in the Father's house. Jesus said,

> *Let not your heart be troubled; you believe in God, believe also in Me. In My Father's house are many mansions; if it were not so, I would have told you. I go to prepare a place for you. And if I go and prepare a place for you, I will come again and receive you to Myself; that where I am, there you may be also. And where I go you know, and the way you know.* (John 14:1–4)

Cool! So when we are saved, Jesus prepares a place for us to live with Him in heaven.

You Get Answered Prayer

Take a look at the following three statements made by Jesus:

> *Most assuredly, I say to you, he who believes in Me, the works that I do he will do also; and greater works than these he will do, because I go to My Father. And whatever you ask in My name, that I will do, that the Father may be glorified in the Son. If you ask anything in My name, I will do it.* (John 14:12–14)

> *You did not choose Me, but I chose you and appointed you that you should go and bear fruit, and that your fruit should remain, that whatever you ask the Father in My name He may give you.* (John 15:16)

> *And in that day you will ask Me nothing. Most assuredly, I say to you, whatever you ask the Father in My name He will give you. Until now you have asked nothing in My name. Ask, and you will receive, that your joy may be full.* (John 16:23–24)

Jesus is telling us that God will answer our prayers (a) if we believe in Jesus, (b) if we glorify the Father, (c) if we ask in Jesus name, and (d) if we bear fruit. (No, you don't have to bring God apples, oranges, or pears. It means producing results for the kingdom of God.) So it is not a blank check as many people like to believe. You can't pray that God will drop a brick on your neighbor's head. That doesn't meet the criteria. He is saying that if you are living according to God's will, then He will grant your prayers because your prayers will be for God's will to be done! And as I said earlier, God does answer our prayers, but not always when we want and how we want.

You get Persecution

Darn, all the other stuff is really good. Why did He have to throw in this one? In John 15:20–24 Jesus says,

> *If the world hates you, you know that it hated Me before it hated you. If you were of the world, the world would love its own. Yet because you are not of the world, but I chose you out of the world, therefore the world hates you. Remember the word that I said to you, "A servant is not greater than his master." If they persecuted Me, they will also persecute you. If they kept My word, they will keep yours also. But all these things they will do to you for My name's sake, because they do not know Him who sent Me. If I had not come and spoken to them, they would have no sin, but now they have no excuse for their sin. He who hates Me hates My Father also. If I had not done among them the works which no one else did, they would have no sin; but now they have seen and also hated both Me and My Father.*

In John 16:1–3 He says,

> *These things I have spoken to you, that you should not be made to stumble. They will put you out of the synagogues; yes, the time is coming that whoever kills you will think that he offers God service. And these things they will do to you because they have not known the Father nor Me. But these things I have told you, that when the time comes, you may remember that I told you of them.*

In John 16:33 He also says,

*These things I have spoken to you, that in Me you may
have peace. In the world you will have tribulation; but
be of good cheer, I have overcome the world.*

So why does the world hate Christ? The world hates Him because
they don't like what He said, because He said that He is the only
way to God. (That is the topic of the next section). The world hates
Christ because the ruler of the world is Satan. Yes, I know that some
of you think I'm crazy when I say that. Jesus said it. Jesus said that
Satan is the ruler of this world, and He meant it. He also said that
Satan is the father of all lies. He said Satan comes to steal, kill, and
destroy. He told the Pharisees, who did not believe in Him but chose
to believe in their own self-righteousness, that their father was Satan
and that he was a liar. The world is deceived by Satan. Therefore,
the world hates Christ. But Jesus said there is good news. He has
overcome the world!

In 1 Corinthians 1:18, Paul said, "For the message of the cross is
foolishness to those who are perishing, but to us who are being saved
it is the power of God."

Lewis says it this way: "Enemy-occupied territory—that is what
this world is. Christianity is the story of how the rightful king has
landed, you might say landed in disguise, and is calling us to take
part in a great campaign of sabotage."

Jesus is the only way to be Saved

Jesus tells us repeatedly that He is the only way, that there is no other.
He tells us that we can't do it without Him, so we shouldn't try.

Jesus is the Way, the Truth and the Life

John 14:6–11 says,

> Jesus said to him, *"I am the way, the truth, and the life. No one comes to the Father except through Me. If you had known Me, you would have known My Father also; and from now on you know Him and have seen Him."* Philip said to Him, "Lord, show us the Father, and it is sufficient for us." Jesus said to him, *"Have I been with you so long, and yet you have not known Me, Philip? He who has seen Me has seen the Father; so how can you say, 'Show us the Father'? Do you not believe that I am in the Father, and the Father in Me? The words that I speak to you I do not speak on My own authority; but the Father who dwells in Me does the works. Believe Me that I am in the Father and the Father in Me, or else believe Me for the sake of the works themselves."*

He said, *"No one comes to the Father except through Me."* This is very clear. It amazes me that so many people will not accept this. They don't like it, so they simply choose not to believe it. For some reason, they want to find another way or many other ways. I've had people tell me this is too exclusive. It's not exclusive. Jesus will accept anyone who believes in Him. In John 6:37, Jesus said, *"And the one who comes to Me I shall by no means cast away."* The thing is that many people don't like the fact that you must believe in Jesus to get to the Father. We have friends who are nice people, who are Buddhists, Hindus, Muslims, Jews, atheists, etc., and we want them to be okay. We want them to go to heaven. We want God to accept people who reject Jesus. Jesus said that is just not going to happen.

We just read Jesus's statement, *"I am in the Father and the Father in Me,"* and in John 10:30, Jesus states, *"I and the Father are one,"* so if you reject Jesus, you are rejecting God the Father. It's that simple. He also says in John 5:22–23, *"For the Father judges no one, but has committed all judgment to the Son, that all should honor the Son just as they honor the Father. He who does not honor the Son does not honor the Father who sent Him,"* and in John 15:23, Jesus says, *"He who hates Me hates My Father also."* So according to Jesus, if you want God the Father, you must get to Him by believing and receiving Jesus Christ. There is no other way.

Jesus is the door to salvation

John 10:7–18 says,

> Then Jesus said to them again, *"Most assuredly, I say to you, I am the door of the sheep. All who ever came before Me are thieves and robbers, but the sheep did not hear them. I am the door. If anyone enters by Me, he will be saved, and will go in and out and find pasture. The thief does not come except to steal, and to kill, and to destroy. I have come that they may have life, and that they may have it more abundantly. I am the good shepherd. The good shepherd gives His life for the sheep. But a hireling, he who is not the shepherd, one who does not own the sheep, sees the wolf coming and leaves the sheep and flees; and the wolf catches the sheep and scatters them. The hireling flees because he is a hireling and does not care about the sheep. I am the good shepherd; and I know My sheep, and am known by My own. As the Father knows Me, even so I know the Father; and I lay down My life for the sheep. And other sheep I have which*

are not of this fold; them also I must bring, and they will hear My voice; and there will be one flock and one shepherd.

Jesus said, *"If anyone enters by Me, he will be saved."* He said all others are thieves and robbers and that they come to steal, kill, and destroy. All the false prophets come to steal, kill, and destroy. I'll say it again. All the other religions—Buddhists, Hindus, Muslims, Unitarians, Scientologists, etc.—all teach contrary to the teaching of Jesus Christ. *All of them* are thieves and robbers, all sent to steal, kill, and destroy your very soul. And they will be really nice to you while they do it. Of course they do not have bad intentions. They believe their own religion is correct. But if they are correct, then Jesus is a liar. Yes, it is that black and white. There is no in between. Jesus said you are either with Him or you are against Him. And Jesus points out that His sheep do not hear the 'thieves and robbers.' They only hear His voice. He laid down His life for the sheep. Also note that He said there are other sheep (Gentiles) and that He will bring them in. They will hear his voice, and there will be one flock (the Church) and one Shepherd (the Christ).

Then the Jews asked Jesus if He is the Christ. John 10:24–30 says,

Jesus answered them, *"I told you, and you do not believe. The works that I do in My Father's name, they bear witness of Me. But you do not believe, because you are not of My sheep, as I said to you. My sheep hear My voice, and I know them, and they follow Me. And I give them eternal life, and they shall never perish; neither shall anyone snatch them out of My hand. My Father, who has given them to Me, is greater than all; and no one is able to snatch them out of My Father's hand. I and My Father are one."*

He told them, but they didn't believe because they were not His sheep. His sheep hear His voice, and they follow Him. Then He says that He and the Father are one, not two separate beings. Yes, I know that there are some Christian sects who do not believe this. They don't think He really meant it. They think it was just figurative, not literal. Jesus said it, and I literally believe it. Yes, I believe in the Holy Trinity—God the Father, God the Son, and God the Holy Spirit—and when you are saved, they make their home in you just like Jesus said. Lewis describes the Holy Trinity as God the Spirit dwelling inside you, God the Son walking beside you, and God the Father above you (Lewis, 1952). I think it is a good way to understand it.

Jesus is the True Vine

In John 15:1–8 Jesus says,

> *I am the true vine, and My Father is the vinedresser. Every branch in Me that does not bear fruit He takes away; and every branch that bears fruit He prunes, that it may bear more fruit. You are already clean because of the word which I have spoken to you. Abide in Me, and I in you. As the branch cannot bear fruit of itself, unless it abides in the vine, neither can you, unless you abide in Me. I am the vine, you are the branches. He who abides in Me, and I in him, bears much fruit; for without Me you can do nothing. If anyone does not abide in Me, he is cast out as a branch and is withered; and they gather them and throw them into the fire, and they are burned. If you abide in Me, and My words abide in you, you will ask what you desire, and it shall be done for you. By this My Father is glorified, that you bear much fruit; so you will be My disciples.*

Jesus tells us to abide in Him, and we will bear much fruit as a result; however, without Him, we can do nothing. I find this very true in my own life. If I try to do good and to help others on my own, it doesn't work out, but if the Holy Spirit leads me to someone who needs help or He leads someone to me, then it works. There is a very good book by Bruce Wilkerson titled *You Were Born for This* that explains how you can volunteer to serve God. He will use you by sending you on little everyday missions, and little miracles will occur. It is very true. I have experienced it many times in my own life, and it is a great joy to serve the Lord in that way.

Jesus also says that if we do not abide in Him, we're toast! We will be cast out. We will wither. We will be thrown into the fire and burned. This is another strong warning, just in case we didn't pay attention to all the previous warnings. Then Jesus goes on to say that if we do abide in Him, He will grant us what we desire, and we will glorify the Father. By the way, that is repeated theme in the Bible. God will grant us the desires of our hearts for His glory, not for our own. If our hearts are aligned with His, then we are in good shape, and He will grant the desires of our hearts; however, if our hearts are selfish and our desires are not in line with His and do not glorify Him, then He's not going to grant them. If you are abiding in Christ, then your desires will be for those things that glorify the Father. That becomes your goal.

I also want to point out that in verse 2, God prunes the good branches that do bear fruit. This has happened in my own life, and I believe that it happens to all Christians. He will come into your life with some big pruning shears and cut off all the stuff that is no good. He will tell you to get rid of your bad habits, your bad relationships, your wrong priorities, maybe your possessions, and definitely your pride (He doesn't like that at all!). He will tell you to rid yourself of anything that keeps you from having a close relationship with God. You may not like this pruning process. It may be long and painful, but it is necessary. It is good, and when it is done, you will be happier, and joyful in your relationship with the Lord. And you will bear more fruit.

Summing all this up, Jesus is the Door. Jesus is the Good Shepherd. Jesus is the Vine. Jesus is the Way, the Truth, and the Life. No one comes to the Father except by Him. Jesus is the only way. Again He keeps telling us that we can't do it without Him, so don't try.

Unbelief

Jesus said that in spite of this, some people just don't want to believe Him. In John 5:41–44 He says,

> *I do not receive honor from men. But I know you, that you do not have the love of God in you. I have come in My Father's name, and you do not receive Me; if another comes in his own name, him you will receive. How can you believe, who receive honor from one another, and do not seek the honor that comes from the only God?*

John 8:42–47 says,

> Jesus said to them, *"If God were your Father, you would love Me, for I proceeded forth and came from God; nor have I come of Myself, but He sent Me. Why do you not understand My speech? Because you are not able to listen to My word. You are of your father the devil, and the desires of your father you want to do. He was a murderer from the beginning, and does not stand in the truth, because there is no truth in him. When he speaks a lie, he speaks from his own resources,*

for he is a liar and the father of it. But because I tell the truth, you do not believe Me. Which of you convicts Me of sin? And if I tell the truth, why do you not believe Me? He who is of God hears God's words; therefore you do not hear, because you are not of God."

In John 6:36 Jesus states,

But I said to you that you have seen Me and yet do not believe.

In John 5:34–40 He tells us,

Yet I do not receive testimony from man, but I say these things that you may be saved. He was the burning and shining lamp, and you were willing for a time to rejoice in his light. But I have a greater witness than John's; for the works which the Father has given Me to finish—the very works that I do—bear witness of Me, that the Father has sent Me. And the Father Himself, who sent Me, has testified of Me. You have neither heard His voice at any time, nor seen His form. But you do not have His word abiding in you, because whom He sent, Him you do not believe. You search the Scriptures, for in them you think you have eternal life; and these are they which testify of Me. But you are not willing to come to Me that you may have life.

Yes, there are a lot of skeptics out there. There are many people who literally scoff at Christianity and Christians. As you just read, Jesus had some pretty harsh words for them. Everyone has the right to believe what they want, but I think it is good to remember Galatians 6:7, "Do not be deceived: God cannot be mocked. A man reaps what he sows."

I do have a few questions for the skeptics:

1. When people like me, average Christians, say that Christ lives in us, what do you think? Do you think we are lying? Do you think we are just fools who are deceived? Or as I have often heard, do you think we are just weak people with weak minds? (That one does make me laugh.)

2. What do you think of more prominent Christians who claim that Christ lives in them? How about the great preachers—Martin Luther, John Wesley, George Whitfield, Billy Graham? Do you think they were deceived? Do you think they had weak minds? Really? Martin Luther?

3. How about the founders of our country—George Washington, John Adams, Patrick Henry, John Jay, Benjamin Rush, etc.? Do you think they were lying or that they were fools or that they were deceived or that they were weak men with weak minds? How about the founders of the Ivy League schools, such as the Rev. John Harvard? Do you realize that all the Ivy League colleges were founded by Evangelical Christians? What about great businessmen—Conrad Hilton, J. C. Penny, Samuel Colgate, etc.? How about the other former presidents of our nation—Lincoln, Wilson, Roosevelt, Truman, Eisenhower, Reagan? Do you think they were all fools who were deceived? Do you think they were all wrong? Do you think that you are wiser than these men? Of course you don't. That would be ridiculous, right?

4. And do you think that Christianity as the very foundation of Western civilization is all wrong, just an outdated religion for superstitious people? You do realize that at the center of every village in Europe is a church. At the center of every city is a cathedral. The same goes for New England. Do you think that was all wrong?

No, these men were right.

What I will give you is that churches and church people who are calling themselves Christians have often been much less than Christian, not obeying the commandments of Christ, which I have presented to you in these chapters. People have asked me things like, "What about the Spanish Inquisition, the massacres during the Crusades, the witch hunts, etc.?" They cite these as terrible acts done by Christians. Sorry, but these people were not Christians. They called themselves Christians, but Christ did not teach them to do any of that stuff. Actually I'm pretty sure that He was very angry about it! They did not follow His commandments. My point here is that there is nothing wrong with Jesus Christ or God, so don't let bad churches and bad church people turn you away from Christ or from Christianity. I think it's fine if it turns you away from self-righteous, hypocritical religious people, but do not turn from Christ. That would be eternally fatal. Instead, find a good Bible-believing church, go and hear the word preached.

I have been in many Christian churches where I have suspected that less than half of the members of the congregation were Christians. And I have been to some churches where I am not sure that any of them are Christians, including the preacher. They think they are, but they are not. What do I mean when I say that these are people who profess to be Christians are not? After all, they are members of Christian churches. I mean that they are not born again, that they do not recognize Jesus Christ as Lord of their lives, and they are not truly disciples of Christ in that they do not do what He says. In other words, I mean exactly what Jesus meant when He said in the Matthew 7:21, *"Not everyone who says to Me, 'Lord, Lord,' shall enter the kingdom of heaven, but he who does the will of My Father in heaven."*

Some "Christian" churches openly admit that they don't really believe the words of Jesus Christ. In my book, they are not Christians at all. Stay away from those people. That is why it is important to find a *good* church with real Christians, one that teaches the Word of God. Real Christians aren't perfect. They are sinners too, but at least they won't lead you astray with false doctrine. By the way, true Christians are filled with the Holy Spirit, and the fruits of the Holy Spirit are described by the apostle Paul in Galatians 5:22-23, "But the fruit of the Spirit is love, joy, peace, longsuffering, kindness, goodness, faithfulness, gentleness, self-control. Against such there is no law."

What Happens If You Are Not Saved?

Well, that is pretty simple. According to John 8:23–24, Jesus said that you will die in your sins. "And He said to them, *'You are from beneath; I am from above. You are of this world; I am not of this world. Therefore I said to you that you will die in your sins; for if you do not believe that I am He, you will die in your sins.'*"

He also said in John 3:18, "*He who believes in Him is not condemned; but he who does not believe is condemned already, because he has not believed in the name of the only begotten Son of God.*" So you die in your sins, and you are condemned by God!

In John 3:36, Jesus said, "*He who believes in the Son has everlasting life; and he who does not believe the Son shall not see life, but the wrath of God abides on him.*" As I mentioned earlier, having the wrath of God abide on you sounds very painful to me.

And how is this wrath to be manifested upon you? Well, in John 15:6, Jesus said, "*If anyone does not abide in Me, he is cast out as a branch and is withered; and they gather them and throw them into the fire, and they are burned.*" You may recall Jesus' many previous warnings about the fire.

So to sum it up, Jesus said that if you are not born again by believing in Him and accepting Him as your Savior, then you will not be forgiven. Instead, you will die in your sins. You will also be condemned, and the wrath of God will abide on you. Finally, you will be cast into the fire and burned.

Once again, I remind you that it is Jesus Christ saying these things, not me, not some crazy preacher, not some religious nut job, just Jesus Christ Himself. I believe He meant what He said.

Oh, and remember that this is true of everyone, even if you think you are a good person. Guess what? You're not. Jesus said that too. *"No one is good but One."* (Matthew 19:17) And in 1 John 1:10, John states, "If we say that we have no sin, we deceive ourselves, and the truth is not in us. If we confess our sins, He is faithful and just to forgive us our sins and to cleanse us from all unrighteousness. If we say that we have not sinned, we make Him a liar, and His word is not in us."

So based on all this, if you have not accepted Christ and been born again, it is my strong recommendation that you seek Jesus now and become born again. You know, so that you get all those cool benefits of actually having a relationship with God. As an additional perk, you avoid the fire.

If you have not been born again, I hope that you find a certain urgency in all of this. If this discussion makes you uncomfortable, that's probably a very good thing. Billy Graham was known for ending his sermons by saying things like, "Now is the time for salvation. Don't wait. You could die tomorrow." He has a good point.

Similarly C. S. Lewis said, "Now, today, this moment, now is our chance to choose the right side. God is holding back (judgment) to give us a chance. It will not last forever. We must take it or leave it." (Lewis, 1952)

CHAPTER 4

The Redemption

Jesus said, *"I have come that they may have life,
and that they may have it more abundantly."*
—JOHN 10:10

So what was the result of all of this—the mold, the illness, the financial and material loss, the personal loss, the chastisement? It was the best thing that could have happened in my life! It brought me back to the Lord and renewed my relationship with Him. I now make it my priority to put God first in my life, to obey the first and greatest commandment, and to live Matthew 6:33, which says, *"But seek first the kingdom of God and His righteousness, and all these things shall be added to you."*

I am now happier than ever as I enjoy having a relationship with God, spending time with Him in prayer, walking with Him throughout the day, and listening to His voice. I am enjoying the fruits of the Holy Spirit described by the apostle Paul in Galatians 5:22-23.

Reading, and rereading Matthew and John set me straight and put me back on the right track in terms of how to live my life and how to save my soul. I am now living the life that God meant for me and that is a wonderful thing.

THE PAIN STOPPED!

So I recommitted my life to the Lord, and eventually the suffering stopped. It didn't happen overnight. The pain and suffering continued for about eighteen months after I started all this prayer and supplication. God did not heal me. Instead, He gave me a solution.

Several times during my illness, I went to visit my parents in Ocala, Florida, usually for about one week during the holidays. I would spend almost all of my time outdoors in the hot sun, and each time I felt much better than I did in Rochester. After about one week my symptoms would start to abate. Then I would go back to Rochester, and in less than one day I would feel terrible again. After I did this four or five times, I decided to try it for one month, so in March of 2012 I took my laptop and cell phone and set up a temporary office on my parent's patio and worked from Florida for one month. It was amazing! After two weeks I was feeling pretty good and working full eight-hour days. After one full month I was perfectly healthy. All my symptoms were gone. I went back to Rochester, thinking I was now healed and looking forward to getting back to work and being productive again.

That didn't happen. I returned to Rochester, very excited to let everyone know that I was healed, but within sixteen hours I was coughing badly again. Within two days all my symptoms had returned and were once again debilitating. I was crushed! I wanted so badly to stay at work. The company needed me. My kids needed me to help support them. I had been toughing it out for almost two years, and I had thought it was finally over, that I was finally healed;

however, I wasn't. I spent the next month getting worse and worse. The pain in my head was excruciating. I needed to do something.

I had read Glenn Beck's book *Being George Washington.*[17] George Washington had a tendency to put himself in harm's way. When he led his men into battle, he led from the front. After one battle he found four bullet holes in his cloak and hat, but he had not been hit. While it was admirable that Washington was so brave and put himself in the same danger as his men, he was too valuable to lose— so valuable that if he were lost, the revolution would be lost, and the nation would be lost. Beck writes,

> Washington's men loved him beyond words. Because of this their single greatest fear was that he would allow himself to be killed in battle. That was the only thing that could destroy their nation, the only thing that could destroy their cause … Lafeyette had once said to Washington, "If you were lost, there is no one who could keep the army and the revolution for 6 months."

I concluded that I was no good to anyone sick or dead—no good to my company or my kids or my family or myself. So I decided that I must move to Ocala. The first week of May I announced to the company that I was moving permanently to Florida. By May 6, I had disposed of all my possessions except for one suitcase of clothing and my 2008 Ford Taurus, my laptop, and my phone. I then loaded up the car and drove to Florida. It took me four days, as I was too sick to travel very far in one day.

I threw out the old clothes and traded in the car. Once I arrived in Florida, I bought new clothes and a new F-150 and moved into the guest room in my parent's house. I set up my office on the patio, and it is working out great. It is not ideal for the company, but it is much better than being so sick that I am useless. Here in Ocala, I am perfectly healthy as long as I stay outdoors in the sun. If I go in moldy buildings, I get sick. If I go to the coast, where it is humid and moldy, I get sick. All my symptoms return. So I now live my life on the patio. I'm healthy and strong, and I am very blessed!

Why Florida? Everyone knows that Florida is humid and moldy. This makes no sense. Well, they are right. I actually tried going to the desert several times. My company has an office in the Mojave Desert. I get just as sick there. It turns out that there is a disease called desert fever that is particular to the Sonoran and Mojave deserts and is caused by a form of desert mold. It makes me very ill. So I am content to live outdoors in Florida. As long as I stay in the sun and out of the shade, I'm fine. Sun kills mold.

RELYING ON GOD

God can now talk to me because I am now willing to listen. My ears were closed before. And as the Bible says, some have ears to hear, and some don't. I talk to God every morning and continue thinking of Him throughout the day. As a result, God talks to me through the Holy Spirit as I described in the previous two chapters.

His Wisdom

I have now learned to rely on God, not upon myself. I rely on His wisdom, direction, and guidance. Proverbs 3:5–6 says, "Trust in the LORD with all your heart, and lean not on your own understanding; In all your ways acknowledge Him, and He shall direct your paths."

George Washington Carver said this verse was the key to his success.[13] One of my best friends also tells me that he and his wife include these verses in their morning prayer every day.

This Scripture is so true. God does things that seem to make no sense to us at the time. They are beyond our understanding, but later we see the reason and the wisdom of His ways because His plans are greater than our plans. As He said in Isaiah 55:9, "For as the heavens are higher than the earth, so are my ways higher than your ways, and my thoughts than your thoughts."

We just need to let Him be God and do things His way. If we go along with that and ask for His direction and guidance, then He does give it to us. We just need to be alert and listen to Him. If we ignore Him and choose to go our own way, He lets us do that too, but that is just stupid.

His Strength

I have also learned to rely upon God's strength, not my own. The apostle Paul said in Philippians 4:13, "I can do all things through Christ who strengthens me." That is my new attitude. In 2 Samuel 22:2–3, King David said, "The LORD is my rock and my fortress and my deliverer; The God of my strength, in whom I will trust."

Whenever I get in stressful situations—sometimes daily—I think of these verses and put my trust in God. I still have to deal with the situation, but I ask God to help me do that, to give me the wisdom, the strength, and the courage to deal with the stress. After all, read what He said in Joshua 1:9, "Have I not commanded you? Be strong and of good courage; do not be afraid, nor be dismayed, for the LORD your God is with you wherever you go."

By the way, the first chapter of Joshua holds the secret to a successful life.

> Only be strong and very courageous, that you may observe to do according to all the law which Moses My servant commanded you; do not turn from it to the right hand or to the left, that you may prosper wherever you go. This Book of the Law shall not depart from your mouth, but you shall meditate in it day and night, that you may observe to do according to all that is written in it. For then you will make your way prosperous, and then you will have good success. (Joshua 1:7-9)

So if we are courageous enough to follow God's law and we keep meditating on it and speaking it, then we will prosper and have success. There are many people writing self-help books, telling us how to be successful. God knows better than they do. We just need to follow the commands He gave to Joshua. That's right— commands, not suggestions, not advice.

My Identity

I rely on Him for my identity as well. As a result of all this soul-searching, I realized who I am and who I was meant to be. This all started long ago. I was about twenty-five years old, and I was in graduate school at the Institute of Optics at the University of Rochester. My office was on the fifth floor. It was about midnight, and I was puzzling over a very difficult lens design problem. I was pacing the halls, thinking about it, and I stopped at a large window overlooking the campus. It was a typical Rochester night—cold, snowy, and very beautiful. I stood there looking out the window, pondering this problem. A fellow student named Ben came up to the window and stood there beside me, admiring the view and thinking about the same problem. Ben was a little older and a little wiser than me, and suddenly Ben asked me, "Doug, what are you?"

I responded, "That's a strange question. I'm an optical scientist just like you."

Ben said, "No, you're not. I'm a scientist. What are you?"

Without hesitation, without any thought at all, the answer came from my heart. "I'm a teacher and a horseman."

Ben replied, "That's right. That is what you are, so that is what you should do," and he walked away from the window. I was a little taken back, almost a little offended, as I had fantastic grades, did very well in my studies and research, and felt I was as capable as the other students. Ben was able to look beyond that. He knew my heart better than I did. I just had to hear myself say it. By the way, Ben is a Christian. He knew.

This was enlightening to me, but I didn't really do anything about it. I finished my PhD, and rather than teach and work with horses, I became chief scientist of a small optics company. I eventually became the president of the company and chief marketer. (That is not an official title, but it is part of my duties.)

My point here is that God puts a desire in our hearts to do what He wants us to do, to be what He wants us to be. The wisest career choice we can make is the one God gives us a desire to do. Some people are smart enough to pursue that. Others are not, opting for careers that they feel are more secure and sensible or have greater financial payoff. In reality, God has a purpose for each of us. It is important to listen to Him so that you know what that is. Otherwise, you can end up trying to *find yourself* or doing something that you don't really love. That usually doesn't work so well, and it can be stressful.

A couple years ago I was reading John Eldredge's book *Wild at Heart*, and at some point he challenged the reader to write down "who you are." So I did.

> I am Douglas Scott Kindred,
> son of Thomas and Judith,
> father to Kai and Mitchell,
> president of Gradient Lens Corporation,
> a blessed son of the Most High God,
> a teacher and a horseman
> in the service of our Lord, Jesus Christ.

This may sound over dramatic, but I like it. It is all true. It sums me up, and it all comes from God. This defines my purpose in life. I have had people ask me, "Doug, what is life all about?" Well, this is it, right here. You don't have to look any further. My purpose is to be all those things I mentioned and to do them in the service of our Lord. Done!

His Blessings

I have also learned to rely on God's blessings and to be thankful for them. One day in November of 2011 I was miserable with my mold illness. I was in a great deal of pain and wanted to die just to alleviate the intense pain. I was driving home from work rather early in the afternoon to head back to my apartment to sleep another sixteen-hour night. On my way home I heard a sermon by a radio preacher on Psalm 37:4.

Psalms 37:4–6 says,

> Delight yourself also in the LORD, and He shall give
> you the desires of your heart. Commit your way to
> the LORD, trust also in Him, and He shall bring it
> to pass. He shall bring forth your righteousness as
> the light, and your justice as the noonday.

As soon as I arrived home, I got out a pen and paper and wrote down the desires of my heart. I did not think about them at all. They literally flowed from my heart like water.

The Desires of My Heart

1. That I walk more closely with God, seek and obey His will, and always do what is right and good. That I share the love of Christ with others.

2. That I find a wife. (Lord, send me the right woman who will be my friend, my partner, my lover, and my wife.)

3. That I be the best father that I can be, that I raise my sons right, that they have full and happy lives, and that they become strong men of God.

4. That I am healthy and physically fit.

5. That I remain mentally fit and morally strong.

6. That I spend more time with my family—my mom and dad, my brother, my sister, and their families. That I may honor and care for them.

7. That I may travel to the mountains and deserts of the west, to Hawaii, to the Caribbean, to Australia and New Zealand, to Africa and Europe, sometimes with Kai and Mitchell.

8. That I live somewhere warm.

9. That I be what I was meant to be, a teacher and a horseman.

10. That I have financial success in order to perform all these items well.

So I prayed that God would grant me the desires of my heart. God told me very clearly that day, "I will bless you in three years." I literally fell off the chair, moaning, thinking that I could not possibly endure three more years of pain and suffering. Maybe He meant that these blessings would be complete in three years. I'm not sure, but two years later the blessings are already starting to flow, and all these things are in the process being fulfilled.

The entire experience has brought me closer to God, which I listed in numbers one and five of my list. I fell in love with a wonderful woman and plan to marry her, which was number two. I moved to Florida and got healthy, bought a nice little piece of land, and plan to build a house there, which speaks to desires number four, six, and eight. I took my sons on vacation to Yellowstone and the Tetons, satisfying numbers three and seven. God has given me the opportunity to share my experiences and share my faith with dozens of people, and I am writing this book. Moreover, a good friend gave me a fine horse, contributing to number nine. The business is growing too, and we have exciting new opportunities, developing number ten. So I feel very blessed and very thankful to God. James was right. "Count it all joy when you suffer trials," and Paul was right when he said that God's grace is sufficient.

DOING GOD'S WORK

John 6:28–29 says, "Then they said to Him, 'What shall we do, that we may work the works of God?' Jesus answered and said to them, *'This is the work of God, that you believe in Him whom He sent.'"*

When I wrote down who I am, you may have noticed that the last line said, "In the service of our Lord Jesus Christ." I took that seriously and started sharing my story with everyone I meet. I also started to write this book, as I felt that God was telling me to write the book. I volunteered to do what He wanted me to do. As a result, sometimes He sends me on a mission. Sometimes God leads me to certain people or leads certain people to me so that I may help them and bless them and vice versa. This is an absolute joy.

God once sent me to a hotel bar in San Diego. Yes, He sent me. I was tired after a long day of work. I went out for dinner and then came back to the hotel, looking forward to swimming and going to bed. I kept hearing His voice saying, "Go to the bar. Go to the bar. Go to the bar." I was arguing with God, saying, "No, I don't want to go," but He wouldn't let it rest. So I went to the bar, ordered a nice glass of sauvignon blanc. Within five minutes a pretty young lady sat next to me, and we enjoyed some fun, flirty conversation; however, then she said something about "principles to live your life by." I said, "I get most of mine from Matthew and from Proverbs."

She looked at me in disbelief, and said, "You believe all that crap?"

Very calmly and with a smile, I said, "Yes, I do." She went on a rant about hypocrites in the church, about how terrible religious people are, about how they are judgmental, un-accepting, unforgiving, etc. She was a disavowed Catholic who had been hurt by all of the scandal in the church. She was actually right about the bad people and the problems with the church, but unfortunately after she left the church, she drifted away from God. It happens all the time. God told me everything to say to her from that point on. It was not me speaking. It was the Holy Spirit speaking truth through me, quoting the words of Jesus. She became so excited about it that she started writing down every Scripture I quoted and vowed to start going back to church. She needed God. She wanted God, so God sent me to her. I want to make it clear: I cannot do things like this on my own. I cannot choose to approach someone and have it work like that. It only works when God sends me to them or sends them to me.

God has sent me on about fifty of these little missions. It is almost always something I do not want to do, somewhere I don't want to go. I just hear His voice saying "Go" and telling me where to go. That is all the information I get. Once I am there, I never approach anyone. Someone approaches me and starts the conversation, and it becomes immediately clear that I was sent to help the person. Then I share with the individual whatever the Holy Spirit leads me to say. It has been a wonderful blessing.

In regard to serving Him, Jesus said in John 12:26, *"If anyone serves Me, let him follow Me; and where I am, there My servant will be also. If anyone serves Me, him My Father will honor."*

In John10:10, Jesus said, *"I have come that they may have life, and that they may have it more abundantly."* That is exactly what I got!

APPENDIX A

Exodus 20—The Ten Commandments

And God spoke all these words, saying: "I *am* the LORD your God, who brought you out of the land of Egypt, out of the house of bondage."

FIRST COMMANDMENT—"You shall have no other gods before Me."

SECOND COMMANDMENT—"You shall not make for yourself a carved image—any likeness *of anything* that *is* in heaven above, or that *is* in the earth beneath, or that *is* in the water under the earth; you shall not bow down to them nor serve them. For I, the LORD your God, *am* a jealous God, visiting the iniquity of the fathers upon the children to the third and fourth *generations* of those who hate Me, but showing mercy to thousands, to those who love Me and keep My commandments."

THIRD COMMANDMENT—"You shall not take the name of the LORD your God in vain, for the LORD will not hold *him* guiltless who takes His name in vain."

FOURTH COMMANDMENT—"Remember the Sabbath day, to keep it holy. Six days you shall labor and do all your work, but the seventh day *is* the Sabbath of the LORD your God. *In it* you shall do no work: you, nor your son, nor your daughter, nor your male servant, nor your female servant, nor your cattle, nor your stranger who *is* within your gates. For *in* six days the LORD made the heavens and the earth, the sea, and all that *is* in them, and rested the seventh day. Therefore the LORD blessed the Sabbath day and hallowed it."

FIFTH COMMANDMENT—"Honor your father and your mother, that your days may be long upon the land which the LORD your God is giving you."

SIXTH COMMANDMENT—"You shall not murder."

SEVENTH COMMANDMENT—"You shall not commit adultery."

EIGHTH COMMANDMENT—"You shall not steal."

NINTH COMMANDMENT—"You shall not bear false witness against your neighbor."

TENTH COMMANDMENT—"You shall not covet your neighbor's house; you shall not covet your neighbor's wife, nor his male servant, nor his female servant, nor his ox, nor his donkey, nor anything that *is* your neighbor's."

REFERENCES

1) Jeremiah, David. "The Danger of Drifting." *Turning Point for God*. Santa Ana, Calif.: Trinity Broadcasting Network, 2012

2) Graham, Franklin, and Donna Lee Toney. *Billy Graham in Quotes*. Nashville, Tenn.: Thomas Nelson, 2011.

3) Stanley, Andy. *How GOOD Is Good Enough*. Colorado Springs, Colo.: WaterBrook Multnomah Books, 2003.

4) Comfort, Ray. *God Has a Wonderful Plan for Your Life: The Myth of the Modern Message*. Bellflower, Calif.: Living Waters Publications, 2010.

5) Lewis, C. S. *Mere Christianity*. New York, N.Y.: HarperOne, 1952.

6) LeTourneau, R. G. *Mover of Men and Mountains*. Chicago, Ill.: Moody Press, 1960, 1967.

7) Chan, Francis. *Crazy Love*. Farmington Hills, Mich.: Cengage Learning, 2008.

8)   Platt, David. *Radical, Taking Back your Faith from the American Dream.* Colorado Springs, Colo.: WaterBrook Multnomah Books, 2010.

9)   Stanley, Charles. *How to Listen to God.* Nashville, Tenn.: Thomas Nelson, 1985.

10) Eldredge, John. *Wild at Heart,* Nashville, Tenn.: Thomas Nelson, 2001.

11) Eldredge, John, and Stasi Eldredge. *Captivating,* Nashville, Tenn.: Thomas Nelson, 2009.

12) Graham, Billy. *The Journey.* Nashville, Tenn.: Thomas Nelson, 2006.

13) Lee, Richard G. *In God We Still Trust.* Nashville, Tenn.: J. Countryman, a division of Thomas Nelson, 2010.

14) Zacharias, Ravi. *Why Jesus?* New York, NY.: FaithWords, 2012.

15) Wilkinson, Bruce. *You Were Born for This.* Colorado Springs, Colo.: WaterBrook Multnomah Books, 2009.

16) Driscoll, Mark, and Gary Breshears. *Vintage Jesus.* Wheaton, Ill.: Crossway Books, 2007.

17) Beck, Glenn, and Kevin Balfe. *Being George Washington.* New York, NY: Threshold Editions/Mercury Radio Arts, a division of Simon and Schuster, 2011.

Printed in the United States
By Bookmasters